ASK THE

GIRL NEXT DOOR

Sexy Answers to Your
Most Intimate Questions

NICOLE BELAND

RODALE

© 2003 by Nicole Beland

Printed in the United States of America
Rodale Inc. makes every effort to use acid-free , recycled paper.

Book Design by Tara Long

Library of Congress Cataloging-in-Publication Data
Beland, Nicole.
    Ask the Men's health girl next door : sexy answers to your most intimate questions / Nicole Beland.
        p.   cm.
Includes index.
    ISBN 1–57954–712–5 paperback
1. Sex instruction for men.   2. Single women—Sexual behavior.
3. Single women—Psychology.   4. Dating (Social customs).
5. Man-woman relationships.   I. Men's health (Magazine)   II. Title.
    HQ36 .B45   2002
    306.7—dc21   2002014800

Distributed to the book trade by St. Martin's Press

2   4   6   8   10   9   7   5   3   1   paperback

Visit us on the Web at www.menshealthbooks.com, or call us toll-free at (800) 848-4735.

WE **INSPIRE** AND **ENABLE** PEOPLE TO IMPROVE
THEIR LIVES AND THE WORLD AROUND THEM

CONTENTS

ACKNOWLEDGMENTS

Big props to Stephen Perrine, editorial creative director of *Men's Health* magazine for creating the "Ask the Girl Next Door" column and recruiting me to write it. Thanks to him and David Zinczenko, *Men's Health* magazine editor-in-chief, for giving me this incredibly fun opportunity, and for putting out a men's magazine that knows how to treat a woman.

Thanks also to Jeremy Katz, executive editor of Rodale *Men's Health* Books, for his enthusiasm for this project; Debbie Pedron and Deanna Portz for their thorough research; and Leah Flickinger for being such a wonderfully supportive and skilled editor.

INTRODUCTION

The first time I helped a guy through a sticky girl-related situation was freshman year in high school. My friend Justin called one afternoon: "Nic, I need to take off your bra."

I was speechless. And his sober, distressed tone made the request sound even more bizarre. Justin had been one of my best friends since kindergarten. But we were close in that split-a-pizza-and-liter-of-coke kind of way—not the let-me-take-your-bra-off kind of way.

I could hear him start to hyperventilate into the receiver. "I'm hanging out with Betsy tonight and she's going to expect me to know how to unhook her bra! What am I gonna do?"

Betsy, a junior, had picked Justin out of the crowd of fresh meat to be her new boyfriend—only she had no idea how clueless he was about girls. So I invited him over and, after fastening one of my Maidenforms around an overstuffed pillow, taught him how to unhook it with one hand. Once we'd reviewed a few French-kissing strategies for good measure, he walked away feeling like a 15-year-old stud. I felt pretty good about myself. And Betsy? She had a big smile on her face the next day at school.

That was just the first of many times when guys have trusted me with their sex and relationship troubles. Maybe it's because I've never minded talking about personal and embarrassing topics. Maybe it's because I understand that dealing with the opposite sex is complicated no matter how intelligent or sensitive or in tune with women you are. Maybe it's because I'm simply not surprised by much. Whatever the case, I've never shied away from calling things like I see them.

That's what the *Men's Health* magazine column "Ask the Girl Next Door" and this book are all about: no-nonsense answers to all your questions about women, from a girl who doesn't hold back when it comes to talking about sex and dating but who still wants the same loving, trusting relationship with a guy—and eventually marriage and kids—most other chicks want.

Am I the proverbial Girl Next Door? Yes—or about as close as you can get and still be a writer living in New York City. Think of me as a spokesperson for all the women you see every day at parties, in bars and clubs, at the office, the gym, the video store, the coffee shop. True, I can't possibly know what's on the mind of every woman out there, but I'm probably right 95 percent of the time. Not just because I have so many smart, sexy 20-something girlfriends to consult with, but also because I've been an editor at both *Cosmopolitan* and *Mademoiselle* magazines, where I spent years researching and writing about every aspect of a woman's life—from makeup to masturbation.

I've culled the questions in this book from the thousands guys have submitted to *Men's Health* since the column first ran in September 2001. And I've chosen them because they're either universal ("What does a women expect the first time in bed?") or specific but pertinent ("I want to break up with a woman, but we work in the same office. How can I make this as painless as possible?"). Whenever I wasn't completely sure how most women feel about an issue, I got my girlfriends together—or, after midnight the day before a deadline, I called my best friend Liesa or my sister Jenai—and we debated the question until we found consensus.

Throughout the questions and answers I've interspersed cool statistics and survey results on everything from what percentage of women enjoy giving oral sex to the number-one gift they want for Valentine's Day. And at the end of every chapter, you'll find eye-opening roundtable discussions where you can "eavesdrop" as I talk with my girlfriends privately and explicitly about what makes a guy sexy, what it takes to make us orgasm, how to keep a long-term relationship hot, and more.

As for me, I love writing "Ask the Girl Next Door." For one thing, I get paid to think about sex. More important, I get the same satisfaction from helping *Men's Health* readers each month as I did the day I taught Justin how to feel up a pillow.

xo,
Nicole

P.S.: I'm more than happy to answer your questions. Just e-mail them to me through www.menshealth.com and I promise to answer as many as I can.

1

THE
GIRL ALONE

**Her Body ■ Her Stuff ■ Her Fantasy Life
■ Miscellaneous Girl Mysteries**

I've always thought women spend way too much time in front of mirrors—getting dressed, putting on makeup, messing with our hair, and worrying about what our butts look like in bikinis. Of course, that doesn't stop me from painting my toenails powder pink and changing my outfit five times before I leave my apartment.

Like all chicks out there, I love girl things. And I catch myself exhibiting other classic female characteristics all the time, whether it's gossiping for hours on the phone with my closest friends, asking a waiter to turn the air conditioner down because I'm freezing, or suddenly realizing that it's just a few days before my period and, wouldn't you know it, my moods have been swinging more than Sammy Sosa. Since every female is at least a little girlie, there isn't much we can do except learn to love that part of ourselves.

As for what it all looks like from a guy's low-maintenance point of view, I can only imagine. But based on the questions men send me, it's clear that most of you are mystified by what goes on in a girl's private life—as you should be. The only guys who aren't probably grew up with five sisters or as the only son of a sorority den mother. For the rest of you, here's why we write in diaries, pooh-pooh three-somes, hoard shoes, and do a lot of other things that don't make much sense to anyone who doesn't have ovaries. Beware: Girl stuff isn't always pretty.

■ Her Body

How often do women have to shave/wax unwanted body hair?

Well, it all depends on how hairy and/or lazy we are. That said, shaving is something we have to do much more often than waxing. Waxing rips hair out by the roots, so it takes longer to grow back and comes in as soft, less visible strands instead of dark, stiff stubble. So if a girl waxes, she probably doesn't do it more than once or twice a month—which is good because waxing hurts like a bitch and has the charming side effect of removing a layer of skin.

According to my unofficial survey of about 30 women at a party, the majority of women shave their pits, legs, and bikini line once or twice a week (much less in wintertime) and wax their upper lip and eyebrows (shaving is a no-no in these spots) once a month. A few said they shave their legs only if they're going to wear a skirt the next day, and others admitted they trim the hedge only if they think an upcoming date might end up in the sack. And here's a bonus bit of info: Three of the women at this particular summer afternoon BBQ regularly shave off *all* their pubic hair. That's 1 in 10!

What, exactly, is a Brazilian bikini wax?

It's extreme body grooming, that's what it is. Put yourself in the pants of a woman who gets one: You lie on your back, naked from the waist down, with your knees tucked up by your ears while a complete stranger—but almost always a woman—powders every square centimeter of your vulva and butt crack (to help prevent skin damage). Then, while pulling at these most intimate parts to access every nook and cranny, she spreads warm wax on your delicate pink flesh and then rips the wax off, taking all the pubic hair with it. You're left with a little triangle tuft in front and not one stray strand anywhere else.

The effect is part Lolita and part porn star, and plenty of women swear by how sexy it makes them feel. The only problem is the upkeep. Pubes start growing back after just 4 or 5 days, but your hairs won't be long enough for another waxing for at least 2 weeks. So after all your trouble (and $50), you end up looking a little messy down there. Why is it called "Brazilian"? Because that's the country where this kind of provocative pubic styling originated.

What happens at a gynecological exam? Do women dread going?

A trip to the gyno is hardly as nerve-racking as a Brazilian bikini wax (see above). And once we've gone to the same doctor a few times, we know what to expect, so it's not really something we dread. Here's how it goes: We strip and put on a standard, front-opening hospital gown, then lie on an examination table. The doc does a breast check first, making small circular motions with the tips of her fingers to feel for lumps. (Trust me—there is nothing erotic about this.)

Then she pulls out the famous stirrups and instructs us to rest our heels in them and scoot down so that our butt is right at the edge of the table. Here's where it gets most embarrassing/uncomfortable: She shines a 300-watt lightbulb directly at our crotch, then lubes up and inserts a speculum (a plastic device that opens up the vagina and looks like two shoehorns screwed together).

At this point the doc does a Pap test, which detects any signs of cervical cancer. Using an extra-long Q-tip, she scrapes cell samples from both inside and outside the cervix. I don't know how to describe the sensation of having your cervix poked—it feels like she could be pricking your liver, say, with a pin. Afterward the cervix will sometimes hurt and bleed a little.

Last, she puts her fingers inside us and feels to make sure our uterus is healthy. We walk out feeling a little exposed, shaky, and vulnerable, but by the time we're leaving the parking lot, the memory has already started to fade.

Do any of your friends have tattoos? Do they mean what guys think they mean: that she's a little wilder than women who are ink-free?

Yes. And yes.

I've noticed that with some women, one breast is smaller than the other. Is that normal/typical?

Yes. Only airbrushed Playmates and females in Japanese anime have perfectly identical breasts. They often hang at a slightly different angle and can differ by as much as a cup size. Boobs may also get bigger and smaller over the course of a woman's menstrual cycle—not so much that you'd notice if you weren't paying attention, but watch closely and you'll see.

P.S.: One of my friends swears that hers swell when they're getting attention from a guy.

Last night I hooked up with a woman whose nipples went in instead of out. What was that about?

They're called inverted nipples. The first time I saw a pair was in gym class in eighth grade when my friend Christine asked if mine were "inside out" like hers. I was probably as surprised as you were last night. They're caused when the milk ducts inside a woman's breasts are a little too short and pull the nipple in toward the chest.

Some women have one inverted nipple and one regular one. Innies don't require any different treatment than regular nipples or cause any health problems, but a girl might be self-conscious about them, so telling her you think her breasts are sexy will likely put her mind at ease.

> Number of women who have more than two nipples:
> **1 in 500**
>
> (SOURCE: *Men's Health* magazine, May 2002)

Sometimes when I'm fingering my girlfriend, I'll get this white, creamy substance on my hand. It doesn't smell or anything, but what the hell is it?

The Average 20-to-29-Year-Old American Woman's Bod
Height: **5'4"**
Weight: **142 lb**
Bra size: **36C**
Percentage of American women who are dangerously underweight: **14**

The Average Playboy Playmate's Bod
Height: **5'6"**
Weight: **115 lb**
Bra Size: **Not available**
Percentage of Playboy Playmates who are dangerously underweight: **70**

(SOURCES: National Center for Health Statistics; E. Richard Brown, Ph.D., UCLA Center for Health Policy Research; planetpretty.com; playboy.com; *International Journal of Obesity*)

What you've got there is vaginal discharge. And even though it's perfectly normal, there's no way to make that stuff not sound gross.

Let me explain. The color and consistency of vaginal fluid fluctuate over the course of your girlfriend's menstrual cycle and can range from clear and water thin to white and pasty and still be perfectly healthy. It's common for it to get thicker right before her period. A light salty or musky smell is also normal. The only time you should truly be concerned is if the fluid is discolored or smells really fishy, which indicates that she has an infection of the bacterial or yeast variety. If that's the case, you shouldn't really go down on her (yuck!) or have sex with her.

As for what you should say to her if you find something foul, as awkward as it is, there's really no way to, um, beat around the bush. I'd try something like "You seem a little different down there tonight. It's not bad, just different. Are you sure you're okay? I don't want to hurt you or anything." She shouldn't freak out too bad.

CRIMSON TIDE Six Things Your Girlfriend Wishes You Knew about Her Period

You probably don't keep track of your girlfriend's menstrual cycle, but maybe you should. Knowing when Big Red is on the way will help you navigate the PMS minefield and understand the changes going on in her body—changes that have a direct effect on your sex life.

1. It never ends. The typical menstrual cycle lasts 28 days, the first being the day she starts bleeding. The average number of bloody days ranges from 2 to 7. Then nothing happens until the very middle of the cycle, when the ovaries release an egg and some women experience a cramping (and horniness—see below). That's followed by another uneventful week or so, and then PMS symptoms can start as early as 10 days before the cycle starts all over again.

2. It's a libido roller-coaster. During the first 2 or 3 days she's on the rag, don't be surprised if it's harder to get your girlfriend turned on. Between hormone-induced bloating, breakouts and cramps, feeling sexy is damn near impossible. But some of my friends report feeling extra horny when "Aunt Flo" is in town. If that's the case, and you don't mind a mess, you're one lucky guy.

3. It determines fertility. At the very midpoint of her cycle is the week during which she ovulates—the time of the month when she's technically able to get pregnant. The

Can women feel themselves getting wet? What's that like?

When I'm kissing a guy and my body starts to respond, there will be a tingly, aching feeling between my legs, and my vagina

---

female body must really want to start sustaining a life at this point because, as a result, most women tend to feel really randy. If you're looking to plan a sex marathon with your girl, now is the time.

4. It makes her bigger. Most women's breasts feel full (some will swell an entire cup size larger) and tender before and during their periods. But that doesn't mean she doesn't want you to touch them—just be gentle.

5. It hurts. Women often complain about lower-back pain during PMS. Offering your girlfriend a massage at this time of the month will be like offering a broke coke addict a line: She'll confuse you with God.

6. It makes her insane. When she's PMSing, raging hormones will cause her to overreact to things—she'll get pissed off when the waitress doesn't bring the ketchup right away, cry at a Hallmark commercial, become convinced that you don't love her because you arrived 15 minutes later than you said you would. This is not her fault, so please try not to hold it against her. In these situations, hugging can be more effective than talking when it comes to calming her crazy ass down. Chocolate helps, too. If all else fails, make yourself scarce.

(SOURCE: *The Kinsey Institute's New Report on Sex*)

will start to feel hot, sensitive, and sort of slippery. It doesn't feel like liquid is flowing from one point to another. I'm just suddenly wet the way your mouth will go from dry to salivating when you smell your favorite food. Sometimes a girl can be very wet inside, but if you touched just the outside of her vagina, you wouldn't be able to tell. That's because the labia majora, or lips for those of you who failed sex ed, can get in the way of the vaginal opening, keeping the wetness in. A finger or penis gently pushing against the opening will get things slick.

■ Her Stuff

Are bras comfortable? What about G-strings?

Remember your elementary school underwear drawer? The one filled to the brim with dozens of tightie whities that ranged from the skid-marked pair with the shot elastic to the stiff newbies fresh out of their shrink-wrap packaging? Well, that's sort of what a woman's bra drawer is like (except without the skid marks). Any given woman has at least 25 bras, only a few of which fit like a glove and are perfectly comfy. The others have shoulder or back straps that feel too tight, lace that itches, or a metal underwire that cuts into our skin. And some bras don't give enough support, leaving our sensitive breasts to bounce every time we take a step (and that starts to hurt after a while, hence the need for the bra in the first place). The only women whose tah-tahs don't feel tender if left untethered are those whose chests are flat enough to escape the force of gravity.

Percentage of women who own more than 40 pairs of underwear: **40**

Percentage of women who own "special occasion" undies: **65.8**

(SOURCE: Howard Merrell & Partners, Raleigh, North Carolina)

As for G-strings and thong panties, they're like contact lenses—once they're in, you forget they're there.

What do women do with all those products in the shower and bathroom anyway?

Oh, nothing. We all wake up every day with clean, shiny, perfectly sculpted hair (so why would we need shampoo, conditioner, or dozens of tubes and bottles of styling products to achieve different looks?); silky smooth skin (no point in owning half a dozen exfoliating shower gels and moisturizers made specifically for different parts of our bodies and seasons of the year); ruby red lips, movie-star eyelashes, and glowing pink cheeks (which could be faked via drawers, baskets, and/or shelves full of lipsticks, blushes, powders, mascaras, and eyelash curlers); and wrists and necks that smell naturally like fields of daisies or exotic Asian spices (making expensive perfumes or scented lotions redundant). Yeah, so all those products? They're just for show!

I read somewhere that women end up eating 7 pounds of lipstick over the course of their lives. It smudges, stains the rims of glasses, and gets all over the place when my girlfriend and I kiss. Not to mention, it seldom tastes good. Why wear it?

Because, as with high heels and push-up bras, we've been brainwashed to think we look more attractive and sexier with it on. If you're dating a girl who smears on lipstick every 10 minutes, drop the hint that you want her to stop by saying something like "You look pretty with lipstick on, but even better without." Maybe she'll be relieved to hear that and will stop wearing the stuff.

What do women carry in those huge purses? And then how is it that they sometimes go out with just a tiny little bag and survive?

The really big ones could contain just about anything, but here are some safe bets: cell phone, Palm Pilot or date book, keys, a novel, makeup bag, hairbrush, tissues, CD player and multiple-CD case, several tampons, notebook or journal, bottle of water, a dozen random business cards, $10 in loose change, crumpled receipts, moisturizer, Advil, and a wallet the size of a brick. The tiny bags hold only the bare essentials: cash, I.D., one credit card, cell phone, lip gloss, and keys.

I own four pairs of shoes. But every girl I've ever known has an enormous closet full of them. What's the obsession?

First of all, we women need a lot more shoes than you do. Just because a pair of shoes is formal and black doesn't mean it matches with a formal black dress. Women's fashion is way more precise than that, so we end up needing at least a dozen pairs of shoes just to complete an office wardrobe. Then there are party shoes and weekend shoes and sandals, boots, flip-flops, and sneakers—oh, and that one pair of super-high, extra-slutty heels that you can barely walk in.

The thing about shoes is that, unlike clothes, they're always fun to shop for because it never matters if we've gained a few pounds—our feet still look skinny.

Why do grown women keep stuffed animals on their beds?

Because they're cute, and cute things make us happy.

What are the top five things that women keep hidden in their apartment?

1. A diary
2. Vibrators and other sex accessories
3. Letters from and photos of ex-boyfriends
4. Ex-Lax, Prozac, other embarrassing medications
5. Sappy self-help books with titles like *5 Steps to a Bigger Soul and an Even Bigger Bust*

Why do women keep diaries?

I don't know why we women have the uncontrollable urge to re-gurgitate and analyze every aspect of our lives—but we do, and that's why Oprah is a millionaire.

Personally, I find it maddening to know that all of the mental energy I've wasted decoding past boyfriends' body language, phone messages, e-mails, and offhand comments could have been used to read James Joyce's *Ulysses* three times over. But before I realize it, I'm doing it again. So, to answer your question, a diary is the perfect place to purge ridiculous things like a five-page analysis of a 2-minute conversation; half-baked, irrational, and/or nasty thoughts that you would never utter out loud; junk-food confessions; self-help pep talks; and also sweet, wonderful memories we'll want to read about 10 years from now.

And while we're on the topic, if you ever come across your girlfriend's diary, I beg you—for her sake and yours—not to read it. It's an intellectual and emotional trash can, and no woman should be held responsible for what's in there.

■ Her Fantasy Life

How often do women fantasize about sex?
Who, what, where, et cetera?

I'll bet we think about sex way more often than you think we do. So many things can set us off: soaping up in the shower, pulling on our stockings, feeling the subway seat vibrate, or just getting flashbacks of what happened last night. And when our sexual antennae perk up, our minds naturally wander to our current lover.

Don't get me wrong; we also fantasize about male celebs, or faceless male and female bods going at it every which way they can, and then there's the sexy stranger sneaking into our bedroom. But since the majority of women view great sex as an intimate and emotional experience, it makes sense that our most satisfying, in-depth fantasies involve the man who riles us up for real. In our twisted minds we'll dress you up in medieval armor, have sex with you in an antigravity chamber, get tied up and spanked by you, go down on you in the middle of a costume ball with nothing on but a corset and mask, ride you on the back of a horse and—my favorite—on a raft in the middle of a lake at midnight with a full moon and dolphins jumping over our heads.

What? Your fantasies are never cheesy?

Do straight women ever fantasize about other women?

Yes, although most women feel kind of funny about it afterward. We don't picture anything as *Playboy*-esque as Angelina Jolie covered in whipped cream (although I just did). It's more like fantasizing about a woman as part of an attractive couple (or three or foursome, depending on our moods) going at it. I've also heard women confess that they sometimes imagine fooling around with one of their sexier female friends. I've tried to do that before but find it much easier to picture strangers doing kinky things than women I know. When I try to conjure up a girlfriend's face in ecstasy, she immediately raises a fantasy eyebrow and says, "Eeeew! What the hell are you doing?"

THEY'RE OH-SO-DREAMY | Male Stars We Fantasize about Most

Who: Tom Cruise
Why: Tom is the ultimate boyfriend next door. He's good-looking, but not so flawless that we'd be too intimidated to approach him at a party. And that big, warm smile makes him seem friendly and fun.

Who: Brad Pitt
Why: Brad comes off as a dangerous, gorgeous bad boy who we wouldn't actually want for a long-term boyfriend (how could you ever trust him?) but wouldn't mind having a hot and heavy summer fling with.

Who: Mel Gibson
Why: Mel gives off the kind of knight-in-shining-armor vibe that fuels women's romantic fantasies. We imagine him as honest, brave, wise, and completely devoted to one woman for life. He's the ideal husband.

Why aren't girls into threesomes?

You've probably heard that for women the best sex is emotionally intimate and meaningful, and that's 100 percent true. A threesome might be fun, kinky, and exciting, but it doesn't usually have much to do with deep emotions. And it doesn't pack the he-wants-me-and-only-me punch that most women are looking for. Also, because a threesome is a stereotypical male fantasy, a woman might feel she's being used or taken advantage of if she agrees to one.

In my opinion, threesomes don't pay off beyond the superficial thrill simply because it's too difficult to be a good lover to two people at the same time. In the concise words of George Michael: Sex is best when it's one on one.

Do women secretly fantasize about sleeping with their guy friends?

It'll definitely cross our minds—especially if we just got dumped and are halfway through a pitcher of margaritas. (If we're all the way through the pitcher, it might actually happen.) It's also not unheard of for casual sex between friends to lead to a great relationship.

Do you check out guys'/women's bodies and/or think about sex at the gym?

Mostly I toss cursory glances at both men and women to see who's buff, who's not, and how I compare. But it's kind of hard just to stare at someone without looking like a freak. That said, the other day I was running on a treadmill across from a woman on a stairclimber and I couldn't take my eyes off her. She was wearing a white shirt that you could see her nipples through, her eyes were closed (which is why I could keep watching her), and her mouth was half open. She was dripping in sweat. It was pretty erotic, and I couldn't believe that a crowd of guys hadn't formed around her to see the show. She didn't turn me on, exactly, but she did get my attention. Another time I saw an 80-year-old guy's testicles because they were hanging out of his short shorts on the exercise bike. But that doesn't count because it was an accident.

Honestly, I don't go to the gym to ogle men, but I will let my eyes linger on a particularly great bod. And if I'm thinking about sex, it's usually when I let my mind wander while I'm running, and then I'll drum up some amazing memory of sex with my boyfriend and replay every second in my head.

Do women masturbate a standard way?

Not really, but once a woman finds one or two ways that work for her, she usually sticks with them. For a long time my college roommate thought her favorite method—lying down on her stomach and slipping both hands between her legs to rub her clitoris while rocking her pelvis up and down to add momentum and pressure— was original. Then we saw the live concert video for "Like a Virgin" on MTV and, what do you know, there was Madonna, flipped facedown on a big velvet-covered bed, pulling the same exact move!

How often the average woman masturbates: **Once a week**

(SOURCE: *Men's Health* magazine, May 2002)

Women with very sensitive clitorises can have an orgasm just by pointing the stream of water from a showerhead in the right spot. Others need a high-powered vibrator to stimulate them enough to climax. One friend likes to straddle a towel-covered corner of her kitchen table and rub her clitoris back and forth until she comes. (Trust me, it was not easy to get my friends to admit these things.)

Any way to create some friction on your crotch—I've heard rumors about chicks who can orgasm just by rubbing their thighs together—has pleasure potential. Aren't girls lucky?

Why don't girls watch porn?

A lot of women just never really consider it. It's a "guy thing," so they feel like they're not supposed to watch it, assume they won't like it, and since they already get pretty insecure when comparing themselves with clothed models in fashion magazines, the thought of competing with grapefruit-breasted, flat-stomached porn stars can be confidence shattering.

As for myself and my friends who have seen X-rated stuff, we have a hard time getting into it because it's so obvious that the women are faking their pleasure. We prefer to read erotic novels to get in the mood (studies have shown that men are much more visually oriented than women). But, for your information, a few of my friends do watch porn. And report liking it very much.

■ Miscellaneous Girl Mysteries

My friends and I always joke about how women are way more complicated than men. Would you agree?

Yes. And after hashing it out with my sister for an hour, we decided it has a lot to do with the fact that women want everything to be perfect, and that makes us more demanding, critical, and analytical of ourselves and other people (especially our boyfriends and husbands). Then, when things turn out less than perfect—which they always do—we end up disappointed and upset. It's a vicious cycle.

So why do we strive to get everything just right? Our guess is that because women were still second-class citizens just a few generations ago, we're not as confident and secure about our ability to control things as you guys are. So we simply obsess and worry more.

It doesn't happen often, but every now and then my girlfriend will cancel plans with me because she just wants to hang out alone at home. What does that mean?

When we go out on dates, we want to feel really fabulous—upbeat, attractive, witty, well-rested, the whole thing—and sometimes we're just not up for it. Maybe all of our sexy undies are in the wash, or we didn't have time to shave our legs or redo our toenail polish. Maybe we have wicked gas from the pizza we ate for lunch, or woke up with a massive zit. Maybe we had a horrible day at work and don't want to take out our frustrations on you.

These things happen, but unless we feel really, really comfortable with the relationship, we don't necessarily want you to know about them.

My girlfriend swears she never farts. She's lying, right? Why do women refuse to admit they get gas?

Of course she's lying! Although I do have female friends who I've known for 5 years or more and still have never caught letting one go (and two were college roommates). Holding in farts is just a normal, if challenging, part of female existence. Your girlfriend is probably afraid that if you knew she could work up a stink that could peel the paint off the walls, you'd find her less attractive.

So would you?

Why are women always cold?

Vanity, that's why. We're always wearing slinky little outfits made out of paper-thin fabric that flatter our figures—but bare our arms, shoulders, backs, and/or legs. Translation: Unless it's 75 degrees or warmer, we're never wearing enough clothes. And once we've gone to so much trouble to look cute, the last thing we want to do is cover up in a bulky sweater or jacket—although we'll happily wear yours because, you know, that's romantic.

In a restaurant, why do women always choose the seat facing the room, leaving us to take the seat facing the wall?

Because it guarantees we'll get 100 percent of your attention.

A 25-year-old friend of mine says she doesn't care whether or not she ever gets married. Is she full of it, or are some women really that indifferent about tying the knot?

There really are women out there who don't want to get married. Ever. However, like most women who trash-talk walking down the aisle, your friend is probably more frustrated than full of it. It isn't that she doesn't want to settle into a long, loving relationship; she's just dubious about the nature of marriage itself. From stressful wedding plans to ugly divorces to the very real fear of ending up like Annette Bening in *American Beauty*, there's plenty cause for skepticism.

Some of these women tend to change their minds after meeting an amazing guy. When you're crazy in love with someone, the idea of making it official—filling a room with your favorite people and making a promise to take care of each other for as long as you both shall live—sounds pretty nice even to a cynic.

Why do women like to talk on the phone with each other so much?

Chatting with our friends is a quick, cheap, legal high with long-lasting feel-good effects and zero risk of withdrawal.

A couple of common scenarios: 1) I just ate a football-size cheese burrito and the guilt is killing me. Calling a bud and hearing about her Ben & Jerry's binge cheers me right up. 2) My self-confidence is deflated because the guy I'm dating didn't call when he said he would. I phone my sister, she convinces me that he's insane if he isn't itching to talk to a brainy babe like me, and suddenly my ego is like the Goodyear Blimp. A girl-to-girl gossip session simply never fails to make us feel comforted, understood, and supported. So why not have them 10 times a day?

What goes down at bachelorette parties?

Once in a blue moon I'll hear about a brazen maid of honor who hires a Fabio look-alike to shake his Speedo-clad crotch in front of the bride-to-be. But for the most part, bachelorette party guests meet for dinner and then hit a cheesy club, where they do endless shots and dance until somebody pukes. During the course of the night, we'll humiliate and haze the betrothed by recalling stories of her most embarrassing hookups, forcing her to wear a cheap hat that looks like a veil, demanding that she ask the bartender to sign her cleavage with a Sharpie, and encouraging underage guys to hit on her because she thinks they're "cute." By the end of the night most girls are standing outside of the club, slurring booty calls into cell phones.

TRUE CONFESSIONS "How I Lost My Virginity"

According to the May 2002 issue of *Men's Health* magazine, the average woman says goodbye to her cherry at the age of 18. I guess my friends are a little more curious than most. Here are a few of their stories.

"Freshman year in high school, my boyfriend and I went to a party and snuck into the master bedroom to make out on the king-size waterbed. We were both buzzed and the next thing I knew, all of our clothes were off and I was the one telling him that I couldn't wait any longer. We did it four times in a row—twice with him on top and twice with me on top. We were naturals."

—Heather, 28

"I was 15 and dying to get it over with, but I didn't have a boyfriend. One weekday afternoon before my parents came home from work, I was swimming in the pool with my best friend, who happened to be a guy. I took off my bikini underwater and swam up next to him. He was totally shocked but got the message and started touching and kissing me immediately. We had sex on the rough, scratchy cement surrounding the pool."

—Caitlin, 23

"The longer you wait, the more it seems to mean, so by the time I was 17 and still a virgin, I wasn't about to do it on some random Saturday night. I made my college boyfriend wait an

I was surprised to overhear a few female friends enthusiastically talking about a guy's butt and abs. Is that typical conversation among women?

Yes. One girl I hang out with makes a hobby out of spotting hot guys and elaborating on the finer points of their physiques. She'll

---

entire year before I finally agreed to have sex with him, on New Year's Eve in an expensive hotel room. It really hurt and I bled a lot. I didn't have my first orgasm until 2 years after that, with a different guy."

—Christine, 31

"It was the summer before my sophomore year in high school and I was living with my dad in London. I met the coolest 17-year-old British guy and we ended up hanging out all summer long, making out in the park, on the street, in the movies, everywhere. The night before I had to fly home, we did it standing up in the stairwell of my dad's apartment building. It happened fast, and just when it started to feel good, he pulled out and came all over my legs. We used his jacket to clean up, kissed each other goodbye, and that was it. I sent him three letters from the United States, but he never wrote back."

—Louise, 26

"The first time I had sex was all-American. It happened in the backseat of a jeep in the middle of a grassy field when I was 17, with a varsity football player. I was wearing my cheerleading uniform and everything—at least I was at the beginning."

—Felicia, 29

say stuff like "Wow, did you see that guy? His abs are *tight*! Oooh, the view is just as good from behind. His chest is like a Roman statue's. He should be in a museum. Damn! I'd wrestle him like a frisky gator." Does she really want to screw all the guys she undresses with her eyes? Well, maybe, but mostly she's doing it just for kicks.

Do women linger around naked in health club locker rooms, talking about men?

Like most of my friends, I get in and out of my gym's locker room as fast as I can. It's hot, humid, and crowded with women spraying so many floral-scented body-care products I can't even breathe. The last time I turned to speak to the 50-something-year-old stranger undressing next to me, I found myself staring at two withered and absolutely nonerotic butt cheeks. Trust me, in spite of what you've seen in pornos, you *do not* want to go in there.

Has a female friend ever suggested that you and she fool around just for the hell of it?

No. But my friends and I have joked about how much easier life would be if we could just be lesbians.

GIRLS OVERHEARD:
Masturbation

The Scene
It isn't easy to get women to talk about self-gratification, so I chose a dark, secluded setting for this girls' night out—a corner banquette at Rialto, a hip downtown-Manhattan restaurant that serves a mean mojito. It's 8:00 P.M. on a Thursday.

The Guest List
Anna, 29, a conservative emergency-room doctor from Philadelphia

Jaclyn, 32, a graphic designer with a wild streak
Sarah, 21, a single, outgoing college grad
Jessie, 26, a shy writer and editor

Me: Okay, ladies, so who does it and who doesn't? Anna?

Anna: I don't do it! I mean, hardly ever. Maybe 10 times in my entire life.

Me: Liar.

Anna: No, really! I guess I've always had a boyfriend so have never felt hard up.

Jaclyn: How could you not? That's like being left alone in a room full of toys and never playing with them.

Anna: Well, if you're so comfortable with it, you confess. How often do you do it?

Jaclyn: Hey, I work from home, so it's easy for me. Maybe once every other day on average. But sometimes I'll do it two or three times a day if I'm bored with the project I'm working on and need a little energy boost.

Jessie: You'll have to give me a lesson because the few times I tried it, it just wasn't any fun. Maybe I'm doing it wrong.

Me: When was the last time you tried?

Anna: Actually it was just last Saturday. My fiancé is a doctor too, and he was working the night shift. I stayed home and rented *American Pie* and, you know, it's just this teen movie that kind of makes you horny. So I whipped off my jeans right there on the couch. It was fine. I mean it felt good, but not great.

Sarah: *American Pie* turned you on? That's hilarious! Do you know how much money people waste on porn?

Jaclyn: No, Sarah, how much money do you spend on porn?

Sarah: Let's just say I have a limited collection.

Jaclyn: Okay, I admit, I own porn, too. I think a lot of women do; they just don't talk about it.

Jessie: That stuff grosses me out. Masturbating makes me feel friggin' lonely, and so does porn. For me sex is all about being with another person. It's not something I want to do alone.

Me: But what if there isn't a hot male body around to satisfy yourself with?

Jessie: Then I just try not to think about sex.

Me: And how can you not think about sex? Is that humanly possible?

Jessie: No, I mean, I think about it, but I just don't see the point in having an orgasm by myself.

Sarah: Um, it's a huge stress relief, for one. And it helps you fall asleep. And it releases endorphins in your body, making you feel pretty damn happy for the next 20 minutes or so.

Anna: Yeah, I think that if I had more free time, I'd do it more often. When I get home after working at the ER, I'm so exhausted all I want to do is sleep. And then during the day there always seem to be more important things to do.

Jaclyn: What about in the shower? You could do it in there.

Anna: Good idea. Maybe I should get one of those massaging showerheads.

Sarah: Those are sweet. I use mine on "pulse." Excellent results.

Me: So who was the youngest person here to start . . . , eh, "discovering her sexual self"?

Jaclyn: I think I must have been 12 years old or something. I used to sit on top of my stuffed animals and rock back and forth.

Jessie: I first tried it around my 20th birthday. Someone gave me a vibrator as a joke gift, so I tested it out. It made so much noise I was paranoid the whole time that my sorority sisters next door would hear it. I couldn't relax enough to come. I threw it out the next day.

Sarah: The first time I did it was probably when I was 16 or so. I had just started having sex and I wanted to figure out what made me feel good, so I would finger myself and rub my clitoris in front of the mirror. Turned out I was much better at it than the boy I was sleeping with.

Jaclyn: Isn't that always the case? I've never met a guy who was better than me.

2

THE MEET
MARKET

At First Sight ■ Pickup Scenes ■
Sending and Receiving Signals
■ Exchanging Numbers ■ Hooking Up

You don't know how many nights my friends and I have gone to a bar or party hoping to connect with a great guy only to spend the entire night exchanging flirty looks with a potential someone but not actually speaking to him. Yes, it's partly our fault. We could do the approaching. But except for a few extreme cases, we're simply not going to. The way we see it, if you're really attracted to us, you'll find a way to start a conversation. And if you're not, why should we risk going over and saying hi?

Contrary to popular belief, you do not have to look like a male model to get our attention or use a pickup line to break the ice (as a matter of fact, please don't). But you do have to walk up and start talking, which takes balls, no question. If you're just as nervous about rejection as we are, learning to read our come-here/go-away signals will take the guesswork out of hitting on a girl. Even if the whole idea of a pickup scene turns you off, you can still successfully meet women just by doing the same things single women do (keep reading to find out how). What I'm trying to say is that this doesn't have to be hard because we want what you want—to meet people, have a good time, and maybe even find someone we wouldn't mind going on a date with.

■ At First Sight

How much do a guy's looks really matter to women?

The next time you're out among a bunch of couples, take a good look at who's dating whom. I'll bet you see plenty of beautiful women with guys no one would call handsome even on their best hair day. That's because we're a lot more concerned with whether a guy is smart, funny, trustworthy, and sweet than whether he could pass for a Tommy Hilfiger model. Of course, when we're out on the prowl, the best-looking guys catch our eye the fastest, but that's attraction in its most superficial, fleeting form. And even then, the average-looking guy who makes us laugh, has something intelligent to say, and shows just the right amount of interest without being pushy is the one we'd rather talk to.

What immediately attracts you to a guy?

When it comes to first impressions, the guy who catches my eye is the one who acts just a little bit like . . . me. The scenario: I'm out at a slammed bar. I get a beer, check out the jukebox, and opt for a spot in the back, away from the crowd. If I see a guy making the same moves, I'll naturally be more interested in him than the men who pay no attention to the music and seem to enjoy socializing sardine style.

My theory is that if two people are reacting the same way to a situation, chances are they're going to understand each other—and get along better. To test my theory, I quizzed a salonful of single women. An upbeat party girl said she's most attracted to guys who look like they're having a

Percentage of women who want men who are . . .

Intelligent: **79**
Funny: **70**
Attractive: **34**
Athletic: **12**
Wealthy: **6**

(SOURCE: *American Demographics* magazine, April 2001)

great time, while the shyest chick in the place said she finds quiet guys sexiest. So if you want a woman to notice you, my advice would be to pay attention to her social M.O.—the closer it is to yours, the more likely she'll look your way.

A business colleague of mine says that when he wants to go out and meet women, he just puts on his Rolex. Are all women who notice that kind of thing gold diggers?

Most of them, but not all. A few women I know are wealthy themselves and seek a partner from the same tax bracket who shares their appreciation for the finer things. So they look for things like Rolex watches, Armani belts, and expensive cars as clues that they're dealing with a financial equal. But, yeah, all the others are after his cash.

What do never-been-married women in their twenties think of divorced guys? I'm 32 and recently back on the market.

In the merciless words of my friend Mackenzie, "A recently divorced guy is a no-no. He's on the rebound times a thousand."

The problem is, you're not going to want to get into another serious relationship anytime soon and we know it, so unless we're specifically looking for a casual fling, you might as well have been recently paroled. The good news is that after a year or two, the stigma will start to wear off and you'll have that "experienced older man" thing going for you. Also, after a year or two, many of those "women in their twenties" will be women in their thirties and therefore a hell of a lot less picky.

I'm 5 foot 5 and feel like I have to work harder to impress women. Is it true women would rather not date short guys? What would it take for a woman to date someone shorter than her?

I once dated a guy who was just an inch taller than me, and two of my most attractive girlfriends are currently dating men who are more than an inch shorter than them (Claire is 5 foot 7, and Renee is 5 foot 10). I won't lie to you; women will count a lack of height as a strike against a guy they've just met, but if he's got enough going for him in other departments, they get past it fast.

As for what it would take to get a taller babe into you, that's easy: Be awesome (that is, smart, interesting, funny, athletic, and successful—or as many of those as you can manage).

I'm considering growing a beard but wouldn't want it to get in the way of meeting girls. What kind of facial hair do women like the most?

Don't do it, man. By far, women prefer the clean-shaven look. Not only does a smooth mug show you groom yourself on a regular basis but it's 100 times more pleasant to make out with.

Mustaches make us wonder if you're gay or just horrifically out of touch with current fashion, goatees make us think you're a slacker or a meathead, and beards make us wonder what kind of a face you're hiding under all that hair. One thing women do love, though, is a sexy, stubbly five o'clock shadow. I wouldn't recommend trying to maintain that look permanently—too *Miami Vice*. But after work or on the weekends, it looks extremely hot.

What do women think of body hair? Should I get my back and chest waxed? Shave my armpits?

Percentage of women who prefer haircuts like:
Chris Isaak/Elvis (short/retro): **38**
Fabio (long and straight): **8**
Lorenzo Lamas (long and wavy): **8**
Mr. Clean: **4**

(SOURCE: about.com)

Women over the age of 20 are mature and sophisticated when it comes to many things—yet they'll point and laugh at a guy with Chia Pet forearms or a back pelt you could lose an earring in. It's a shallow turnoff, but a turnoff just the same.

For the most part, a little excess chest and armpit hair is nothing to worry about, though I do know guys who trim overactive patches with scissors, and the women they date are none the wiser. Allover torso waxing is a decent option for guys who have ripped bods (it's commonly known that male athletes wax, and if you're hot enough, chicks won't care about the icky in-between stubble stages).

To our credit, those of us who giggle at gorillas on the street will overlook furriness in the men we fall for. So if you're looking for love and want to seem as attractive as possible to the female public, simply wear a nice button-down shirt or sweater and forget about what locks may lurk underneath. By the time a new love interest finds out (I wouldn't recommend disrobing on the first date), she's more likely to deal than squeal.

What kind of man do women value more these days: a sensitive guy who'll take walks with them and make them dinner or the rough-and-tough type who's more traditionally masculine?

My first thought is of poetic, peace-lovin' Jim Caviezel in the movie *The Thin Red Line*, which would indicate that the sweet, sensitive guy is ahead of the game. But then I remember rough-and-ready Russell Crowe in *Gladiator* and suddenly I've changed my mind.

My guess is that women are attracted to both at the same time. That means the guy who goes on about the way the wind moves through the trees *and* crushes bones with his bare hands really has the edge.

Facial features women find most attractive:
- High cheekbones
- A large chin
- Long eyelashes
- Big eyes

Regardless of what he looks like, a man is 50 to 100 percent more desirable to a woman when other women say they like him.

(SOURCE: Michael Cunningham, Ph.D., University of Louisville)

What kind of men's clothing turns a woman on?

The sexiest outfit on a man has to be dark suit pants, a black leather belt, and a tailored shirt unbuttoned at the neck—as if he just threw aside his jacket and pulled off his tie with one hand. I'm not sure why it works, it just does.

What's the single most effective thing I can do to up my sex appeal?

Hit the gym.

We notice when a guy's forearms bulge, when his waist cuts in, when his biceps curve out from under the sleeves of his T-shirt, and when his calves flex when he walks. A great body is one that women want to see more of and get close to. And the fact that you're fit will mean that you have plenty of energy to go all night—or at least be less likely to fall asleep the second it's over.

If I'm going to spend my time in the gym, what's the one body part I should concentrate on to impress women?

Abs.

You could have shoulders as sculpted as Arnold Schwarzenegger's, thighs more sinewy than Jean Claude Van Damme's, and biceps the size of bowling balls, but if you've got the beginnings of a gut, any discriminating woman will think twice before considering you prime boyfriend material. The way we see it, a little excess midriff meat now means one fat, sloppy bastard in 10 years (kinda like what goes through your mind when you first notice her chubby butt). And personally, the thought of a thick slab of flabby flesh hovering in the air above me like a giant, hirsute jelly doughnut makes me want to toss my Trojans and invest in an industrial-strength vibrator.

When asked what the ideal male body should look like, male college students chose computer images with 30 pounds more muscle than they currently had. The image of men that their female peers picked? Bodies with 15 to 30 pounds *less* muscle than the ideal chosen by the men.

(SOURCE: Harvard Medical School study)

The good news is that if a skinny Vinny has pencil-thin limbs and a nearly concave chest, a set of washboard abs will make him sexy in spite of his girlie-man stature. That's because an impossible-to-resist, taut six-pack is a testament to a man's thrusting power, not to mention a rock-hard surface to grind our lower bodies against with reckless abandon.

And because abs are the toughest part of your body to get buff, we'll assume you've got the drive, determination, and focus we look for in our ideal man. So drop that curl bar, get down on your back, and start crunching—the payoff will be worth the pain.

■ Pickup Scenes

How can I meet more single women?

First, let your friends know that you're in the market and want to be set up. Blind dates can be a nightmare, but your buds know better than anyone else who you might get along with/be attracted to. Second, go out as much as humanly possible. Events with fewer than 20 people are ideal—dinner parties, BBQs, group trips—where there's at least one person you know and many you don't. Third, do more things that the kind of women you'd like to meet would do. So if you prefer athletic/outdoorsy women, join a coed volleyball (or softball or soccer) league, take a rock-climbing course, join a biking club in your city. If you like the artsy or humanitarian type, drag a friend to book readings, museum events, photography exhibits, and benefit parties. You might also consider a cooking class—lots of single women there, too. The key thing to remember is: Go out, go out, go out.

I see this amazing blonde every morning while waiting for the subway, and I'm dying to talk to her. What could I possibly do or say to get and keep her attention?

First I should warn you that the subway, like the street, isn't the best place for introductions. Because it's a public space, she'll likely be a little suspicious of anyone who approaches her.

If you still want to try, here's what I would respond well to: Find out about some cool music or nightlife event happening in your neighborhood, the kind of event that people pass out flyers for. Grab a bunch of said flyers, and the next time you see this girl on the subway, say, "You live in this neighborhood, right? You should come check this out." Then hand her a flyer from your stack (she'll think you're somehow officially involved in it), smile, and walk away. If she shows up, great. Casually walk up to her and tell her you're glad she came. If she doesn't, "bump" into her on the subway platform a week later and ask if she ended up going. She'll say no and you can carry the conversation by telling her how it was.

Contrived? Yes. But potentially very smooth.

Are bars the best places to approach women when you're looking for a potential girlfriend?

Absolutely not. I've surveyed scores of beautiful 20-something women about this for 6 months now. Turns out bookstores, independent record stores, libraries, and cool movie-rental places (the kind with more foreign flicks than new releases) rate much higher than bars. On a scale of 1 to 10, the likelihood that a woman would hand her number to a guy who initiated conversation with her in a bar would be a 4. In a bookstore, record store, et cetera, it would be a 7 or 8.

The reasons? The chance that a guy will be smart and interesting is far greater if he spends his spare time in mom-and-pop stores that specialize in cool media. (I don't know why the library works too, but it does.) You also have to be at least a little appealing, say something clever about the book/band/movie we're focused on, and not seem like you're trying to pick us up until the very last second of the conversation when you ask for our number. Still, a 7 or 8 out of 10 is pretty damn good.

Do women actually go out to "get laid"?

Yes.

What kind of nightspots do you and your friends go to when you're looking to hook up?

The destination of choice: a party thrown by a friend—or at least an acquaintance. Get-togethers in people's apartments or houses naturally feel more intimate and comfortable than public spaces, so we tend to be relaxed and open to meeting people.

Plus, our slightly twisted logic tells us that since a guy has already been invited to the party, he's passed an initial screening test. The odds that he's a psycho or a creep are slimmer than if he were just some random dude in a bar. And since we're likely to know more people there, we'll have lots of watchful eyes on us making sure we don't do something stupid.

I'm a quiet guy and never really approach women at bars. Is there any way to get them to come to me?

Women want to talk to guys at bars, even if it's just to flirt pointlessly, so if you provide us with an easy conversation starter, we'll usually take the bait. So . . . you need to be doing or holding something interesting—and being cute doesn't hurt either. (Cute, by the way, is girlspeak for attractive. And you don't have to be good-looking to be cute. Think John Cusack, Jason Biggs, Moby. With them it's not about chiseled features—they just have that warm, friendly look.)

Want to meet more women? Quit your corporate basketball team and stow your golf clubs. Percentage of female participants in the following sports:

Volleyball: **55**

Inline skating: **52**

Cross-country skiing: **50**

Bowling: **49**

Sailing: **49**

Tennis: **49**

Hiking: **48**

Running: **48**

Biking: **47**

Camping: **47**

Softball: **47**

(SOURCE: National Sporting Goods Association 2001 Survey)

Speaking of cute, taking an adorable small dog to a bar will get you more attention from women (and gay men) than you could ever want. The only caveat is that most will be interested in the dog, not you. Less pathetically obvious is being seen reading the latest, greatest, most-talked-about book. Out of genuine curiosity, women will ask you what you think of it. A guitar or other musical instrument could also prompt questions from curious gals.

Apart from props, playing billiards or darts will earn you glances, especially if you play well.

Is there any way to go to a bar alone and still meet women? Or are you automatically a loser because you're out solo?

In order to pull that off you have to 1) dress cool and 2) act even cooler.

My friend Alicia was just telling me about a guy at a bar who intrigued her because he was a "totally normal-looking, cute guy just sitting there, hanging out on his own." It was crucial that a band was playing—she figured he was there to hear the music, not to scope chicks or drown his sorrows. She also judged him based on his outfit. Because he was wearing Diesel jeans, funky black shoes, and a hip short-sleeve button-down that might have been vintage, she assumed he was creative and interesting, as opposed to a lonely nerd.

This guy's attitude was also key. "He wasn't fidgeting or looking around too much. He was just very chill and almost disinterested in the people around him. But then a couple of times he looked over at me and caught my eye. It made me want to go talk to him." Of course, she didn't have the guts and he didn't make a move either, so they both lost out. We decided that the best way he could have approached her was to wait until she went up to the bar for a drink. Then he could have positioned himself next to her and said something simple like "So, are you really into this band?"

Will a woman be less likely to flirt with me if I'm with a coed group of friends?

Yes, definitely. We'll assume that one of the women you're with is your girlfriend. And we'll also worry that the women in your group will view us as a threat and not be very friendly. If you're looking to meet new women, leave your female friends at home.

I'm a 21-year-old college student with old-fashioned values, but I still like to have a good time. I want a girl who is intelligent, mature, and good-looking—and who's interested in a serious relationship, not game playing. Where should I go to meet women like this?

Not at a frat party, that's for sure.

Let me tell you about a curious Catch-22 that plagues the collegiate dating world. Men think women want tough guys who act like total jerks, so even the nicest guys do the asshole act because they figure it will bring luck with the ladies—and often they're right. Even relatively old-fashioned women looking for traditional relationships will pretend to be bad girls because they think that's what men want—and often they're right, too.

So I wouldn't give up on those party babes just yet. That said, I would skip the Greek scene altogether and look for love at lower-key locales. You'll find the more conventional types in the college center or the library at 11:00 P.M., poring over some 200-pound textbook. Ever think about volunteering for, say, Habitat for Humanity? Well, good girls do, so why not play that field? There's also the classroom. Check out the front row. That's where the most focused, mature gals sit so as to catch every word the professor utters. Another place to look is the track at 6:00 A.M. The gals who get up every morning to run are goal-oriented and disciplined.

> Percentage of singles who meet potential dates . . .
> Through friends, coworkers, family: **65**
> At work: **36**
> At school: **27**
> Online: **26**
> At bars or coffee shops: **26**
> At religious events, the grocery store, the library, a bookstore, the gym: **less than 20**
>
> (SOURCE: *American Demographics* magazine, February 2002)

As for the good-looking part . . . well, you might have to compromise on that one.

I just broke up with my girlfriend of 5 years, and I'm way out of practice approaching women. Are there pickup lines that actually work?

If a woman is in the right mood (drunk and horny) at the right time (very, very late) and you happen to have a British accent and look remarkably like Hugh Grant, a cheesy pickup line delivered with razor-sharp wit could work. Otherwise, don't risk the humiliation. The best way I've seen guys break the ice successfully is simply by maneuvering next to a woman, leaning in close, and making a casual comment that piques her curiosity.

Recently, a close friend of mine fell for a guy whose first words to her were "Hey, doesn't that bartender look just like Redd Foxx from *Sanford and Son*?" Another woman I know had a wild one-nighter with a fellow dinner party guest who pointed at the Olestra-soaked chips she was eating and said, "Rumor has it those things take you to gastrointestinal hell and back. Any truth to that?" By keeping it casual and noncliché, you're keeping her guard down. If she thinks you're cute, smart, funny, or interesting, trust me, she won't let the conversation end anytime soon.

There's a woman at work I haven't spoken with much but I'd love to ask out. Considering how complicated office dating can get, is it worth the risk?

Not if you take your work seriously and want to build a reputation as a professional. Unless the two of you have been flirting with equal enthusiasm, I wouldn't just come right out and ask an unsuspecting coworker for a date. If she says no, working together could get uncomfortable fast—especially if she blabs to everyone about how she turned you down.

Percentage of workers who have been involved in an office romance: **50**

Percentage of those who have engaged in "physical affection" at the office: **39**

(SOURCE: 2001 Office Romance Survey by thevault.com)

Still, I know plenty of happily married couples that began dating at work. The key is to start slow, flirt a little more each week, and ask her out only when you're damn sure she's interested. Start by making small talk to find out what she likes. If she's a baseball fan, say, make a point of mentioning last night's game. Then after a few weeks, once you've established a regular chitchat relationship, stop by her office and casually ask if she wants anything from Starbucks—your treat. Let it grow from there.

It's a long and intricate dance, but each step will cement your "relationship" further and will help you avoid rejection, humiliation, and—God forbid—legal action.

Do any of your attractive, successful friends use online dating services?

As recently as 6 months ago, the answer would have been no. But something has definitely changed. I don't know when or how it happened, but Internet dating is becoming okay for cool people. I asked my beautiful and smart friend Katherine why she started doing it, and this was her answer: "Your friends only have so many single friends they can set you up with, and I always end up partying with the same people, so I just wasn't meeting anyone new. I figured that if I was at the point where online dating looked good, there must be plenty of great guys out there thinking the same thing."

■ Sending and Receiving Signals

How can you tell if a woman wants you to approach her at a bar or party?

Easy, she'll keep looking over at you. Unfortunately, we'll often peek at you when you're not looking, so having a friend keep watch is helpful.

Of course, there's a chance she could be staring at you because she thinks your hair looks hilarious, so you (or your friend) also should track her facial expressions and body language. If she's smiling, playing with her hair, and/or exhibiting other flirty behavior, it's probably for your benefit and she's hoping you'll make a move. Even more telling is if she walks past you to the bar or bathroom when the direct route doesn't require it, and throws you a little smile along the way. Consider that a neon sign flashing, "Talk to me!"

How can I hit on a girl I want to sleep with without giving her the false impression I want a relationship?

Plenty of women are up for no-strings-attached action, so why not just skip the song and dance and make an old-fashioned pass? If she's clearly shown signs that she's hot for you, do your

THE CYBER SCENE Online Personals That Cool Women Use

Salon.com/theonion.com/nerve.com/mediabistro.com: Covering news, humor, sexuality, and freelance media respectively, these four sites are hip and smart, and so are the people who read them. They all use the same company to run their personal ads, so no matter which site you access the personals from, you'll be fishing in the same pond.

Craigslist.com: A laid-back, bare-bones, noncorporate community Web site that's caught on big. If there could be an "up and coming" neighborhood online where all the young, idealistic college grads were starting to hang out, this would be it.

Match.com: This is the mother of all mainstream online dating services. The personals on ivillage.com, msn.com, aol.com, citysearch.com, and others all link you right back here. The sheer number of people (3 million members total) guarantees plenty of quality, and since a half-million new members register each month, if you can't find exactly what you're looking for today, simply wait a few weeks and try again.

best Russell Crowe: Look her in the eye and say, "God, you are so attractive. I'm not looking for anything serious right now, but I'd love to hang out with you on a night when you're free." Honesty (combined with a little Hollywood confidence) is more of a turn-on than you know.

She flirts with me like crazy, but when I try something, she says she just wants to be friends. What the hell is she doing to me?

Jerking you around like you're some kind of half-man, half-Slinky, if you ask me (and you did).

Here's the thing: Flirting is a game, not a promise; so don't go trying to collect on it. As I'm sure you already know, we women love to flirt simply for the sake of flirting. It's not always because we're interested. And even if we are interested, we don't always want to do something about it. If she backs off when you come on strong, take it to mean that she really just wants friendship, and leave it at that. Maybe she doesn't know what she wants yet . . . so giving her some space will also help her make up her mind. Ironically, the second you stop trying to get into her pants, she'll probably start trying to get into yours—but that isn't exactly a problem, now is it?

I'm always meeting flirtatious women, but I'm never quite sure they're actually interested. How can I tell?

Wait and watch. A recreational flirt tends to be equally touchy-feely and full of sexual innuendo with male friends, coworkers, the bartender, her doorman— just about any guy she comes across, including you.

So try to observe her in several situations that include other men. If you notice she gives you more significant attention—engages you in real conversation instead of small talk, goes out of her way to stand or sit next to you, always responds to you first if someone else asks her a question at the same time—odds are you're a special interest, not just another chump victim to her charms.

She's into you if she . . .
- Leans forward or touches you during conversation
- Smiles and/or laughs frequently
- Positions her body so that her legs face you
- Tilts her head down and looks up at you
- Fidgets a lot

And NOT into you if she . . .
- Leans back or twists her torso away from you while talking
- Doesn't smile at all
- Faces her legs away from you
- Crosses her arms in front of her body
- Sits or stands very still

(SOURCE: Jan Hargrave, body-language expert and author of *Let Me See Your Body Talk*)

The age-old question: How do I let a friend know I'm interested in her in a casual, confident, and clear way?

Most women can't be around a guy they're interested in without getting all impish and googly-eyed in spite of themselves. So if she isn't sending sexy signals your way, no matter how casual or confident you act, you're setting yourself up for one of those "I like you, but . . ." letdowns. On the other hand, if she regularly throws you come-hither looks and blushes when you tell her she's beautiful, she'll probably be psyched to hear you say something like "How about we go on an official date this weekend so I can start hitting on you for real?" Hey, it isn't Shakespeare, but it is casual, confident, and clear.

I know some women go out to bars and parties looking to hook up, while others are on the hunt for long-term love. How can you tell who wants what?

Sorry, but there's no good way to be sure. When we want to meet men for either purpose, we'll dress sexy, get a little tipsy to boost our courage, and flirt like mad.

Do women notice what a guy is drinking? Do some drinks send more positive messages than others?

Most women do notice and make a few on-the-spot assumptions about you based on your beverage choice. In general, here's what the average bar babe is thinking:

Martini: Martini-drinking males come off as conservative and egotistical, but also sophisticated. It's the classic choice for successful corporate types who are under a lot of pressure and want to take the edge off fast.

Mojito or caipirinha: Trendy international drinks make a man seem hip, discriminating, cultured, showy, and hard to please.

Vodka tonic or scotch on the rocks: These and other manly bar standards say professional and appealingly down-to-earth—you've got taste, but don't need to prove anything.

Beer: Expensive and/or obscure import beers get the same reaction as trendy international drinks. But your average domestic or popular import gives a guy a laid-back, relaxed vibe that most women love.

Daiquiri, piña colada, or kamikaze: Concoctions typically found on a bar menu in Cancun make us think you're either underage or gay.

O'Doul's: Bad news. You're either an A.A. member (too much baggage) or a teetotaler (too uptight). Unless . . . you have a pile of keys in front of you, which means you're the designated driver—and the kind of caring, responsible guy most chicks are looking for.

■ Exchanging Numbers

What's the smoothest way to ask for a woman's phone number?

Tell her you want it for a specific reason based on the conversation you've been having. For example, if you spoke about music, offer to burn her a CD that you think she'll be into. You'll need her number so you can find out where to send it. Or if she mentioned a recent trip to Mexico, tell her you plan to travel there soon and ask if you could call her for some recommendations.

The great thing about this tactic is it doesn't force the woman to decide whether she wants to go on a date with you on the spot, so she's more likely to say yes if she's on the fence.

Have you ever asked for a guy's number or e-mail address when you were out at a bar? What made you do the asking?

Call me old-fashioned, but I prefer to be pursued. I have no problem asking a guy for his e-mail address if we've had a great conversation about something we're both interested in and I sincerely want to talk more about it. But when it comes to those times when I'm actually attracted to a guy, I admit that I'll wait for him to do the asking.

Of course, I will flirt shamelessly to let him know I want him to ask for the number. So I guess maybe I'm not that old-fashioned after all.

What does it mean when a woman gives you her business card instead of her home phone number?

It means she wants you to call her. Handing someone a card is just easier and more graceful than scribbling your name and number on a napkin. Besides, when you have, like 5,000 business cards in a box at work, you're dying to get rid of the damn things.

The other night when I asked for this woman's number, she hesitated, then offered her e-mail address instead. What does that mean?

It could mean one of two things. Either she just prefers to communicate via e-mail, or she didn't want to give you her number because she wasn't that into you (sorry). Think of it from the woman's perspective. It can be pretty awkward when a guy asks for your number—even if you don't want to go on a date with him, you feel like a bitch if you come right out and say no. So offering your e-mail is a polite and easy way to avoid the issue without actually giving up your digits.

The only way to find out what this particular woman was thinking during her moment of hesitation is to go ahead and e-mail her. If she responds in a flirty way, she's probably up for a date. If she doesn't respond at all or sends back a few neutral sentences, she was blowing you off.

How long should I wait to call after getting a girl's number?

Everyone has a theory about this. I say call 2 days later—either late in the afternoon (if she gave you her work number) or early in the evening (if she handed you her home digits). That gives her an entire day to wonder if you're going to call, but not enough time to get annoyed and disappointed that she hasn't heard from you—or to forget why she wanted to talk to you again in the first place.

■ Hooking Up

What are some ways you let a guy know you want to hook up?

Subtlety doesn't go far in a dark, crowded room with music blasting, so I'll sit really close to the guy, touch him a lot, whisper in his ear, and at the end of the night, I'll give him a coy smile and say, "I'm thinking of leaving soon. What are you going to do?"

How do you know when a woman is too drunk to take home?

True, most people are buzzed enough to see double when they hook up, but the way I look at it, if you have any inkling that she's too hammered to make good decisions, send the chick home in a cab. If the thought of having sex with a semiconscious, could-puke-any-second human doesn't turn you off, maybe the words "date rape" will. I've heard horror stories about guys who had sex with a drunk woman who said yes, only to have her swear she said no the second she sobered up. Bad situation to be in, right?

I was hooking up with this girl full steam and I could tell she was into it by the way she was kissing me and climbing into my jeans. But when I went to unzip her skirt, she freaked out and changed her mind. What was she thinking?

If she put on the brakes that suddenly, it was probably for one of the following reasons:
1. She had her period.
2. She has a boyfriend and her conscience took over.
3. She thought all she wanted was a hookup, then realized she might want to date you and couldn't bring herself to go all the way the first night.
4. She just changed her mind.

What do your friends consider deal breakers when it comes to having casual sex with a guy?

That depends on how horny we are. If we could take or leave the pleasure, we can get awfully picky. Here's an abbreviated list of reasons my friends and I have called things off at the last minute:

1. He had a tattoo of Yosemite Sam on his upper thigh.
2. He had B.O.
3. He kept a framed picture of his ex on his bedside table.
4. He had much-used stacks of *Playboy* in the bathroom.
5. His apartment was disgustingly messy.
6. He had three cats.
7. He wore yellow bikini underwear.
8. He had a creepy horror movie collection.
9. He used satin sheets on his bed.
10. He had too many prescription drugs in his medicine cabinet.

What kind of underwear do women really want us to wear?

Boxers or boxer briefs. Not tightie whities, not bikini briefs. As for colors, black, white, gray, and blue are best. Red is risky, but kind of fun. Going commando is an interesting option. We'll think you're unconventional and a little nuts. Which could work in your favor.

If you're hooking up with a girl you met that night, who's responsible for the condom?

The default condom provider is the guy. And, no, this isn't fair.

Is it okay to ask a hookup if she's on the Pill?

Eh, not really. Your question will make her think you don't want to use a condom, which will probably bug her out. And, sorry to sound like your mother, but for your own safety you should always wear a condom with someone you're not in a long-term monogamous relationship with. So really, you shouldn't have to ask the Pill question at all.

Do women expect you to call them after a casual hookup?

Only if we already knew you before the hookup (see below). If you're not a friend, but just a friend of a friend, or someone we might bump into (or hook up with) again, we'd appreciate a friendly e-mail or a short voice mail saying that you had a good time and you hope we're feeling okay after all that fun. No need to say, "Call me back" or "I'll call you later" or anything else that you don't mean.

I recently visited an old college friend for the weekend and we ended up having sex. I'm not sure how to act. What's your advice?

If either of you has romantic feelings (which can happen after you bang a buddy), your friendship is officially changed for better or worse, depending on whether you can deal with this new development. Most likely, though, she's probably hoping the recent fluid exchange won't affect your relationship.

Percentage of women who say they've had a one-night stand: **39**
Of 18- to 24-year-old women who have had one-night stands, percentage who met their hookups in a bar or club: **92**
Cities in which the most people report having had one-night stands (by percentage of people) . . .
Dallas: **85**
Los Angeles: **58**
Chicago: **53**
New York: **36**

(SOURCE: 2CV Youth Research Agency: Harlequin/Blaze Summer Club Survey)

The thing is, a friend is supposed to care about her, so she expects more from you than the average guy—and she'll be twice as hurt if you dis her. You have to call her—no excuses—within 3 days, whether you want to start a romantic relationship or simply maintain the preromp status quo. So pick up the phone! If you're both thinking it was a onetime, purely sexual incident, you may be able to skip the should-it-or-should-it-not-have-happened/what-does-this-mean/blah-blah-ugh conversation. Tell her you had a good time and then shift into usual conversation. If she wants to talk about it further, she'll bring it up. If you do get into an emotional chat, just don't use the words "mistake" or "bad idea," which she may construe as you thinking she's bad in bed.

I work an early shift on Saturday mornings, which always means an abrupt exit from a Friday-night hookup. How can I cut the morning short without being rude?

The easiest and most polite thing is to let her in on your A.M. responsibilities the night before—after you've hooked up and before you pass out. Explain that if she stays over, she'll have to leave when you do, so she might want to consider going home, no matter how late it is. If you're sleeping at her place, before jetting out the door, leave her a note telling her that you had a great time.

GIRLS OVERHEARD:
What Makes a Guy Sexy

The Scene
Hanging out in Central Park on a sunny Sunday at 2:00 P.M. Someone brought a Frisbee, but we're too busy tanning to break a sweat.

The Guest List
Meredith, 26, a magazine editor and sassy Southern belle
Lara, 24, a funky photographer's assistant
Carol, 22, a no-nonsense psychology grad student
Alyson, 29, an art gallery manager and total romantic

Me: Okay, let's talk about what really attracts women to a guy right away. And don't just say "intelligence and a great sense of humor." I'm talking really specific, superficial stuff that gets your attention and turns you on instantly.
Meredith: What about money? Can I say money?
Me: Yes, if it's true. But how do you know a guy has money?
Meredith: If he's wearing an expensive suit that fits him like a glove, designer shoes and a matching belt, a very chic watch. That guy is sexy because he looks put together, in control, confident, and successful.

Carol: So what you're saying is you're a gold digger.

Meredith: But it's not actually the money I want; it's the self-control and confidence of a successful man that's sexy. And the only way you can tell that about a guy the second you see him is by sizing up his style. So what if I think a guy who can buy me a mansion on the coast is sexy?

Lara: She's right. Money and power definitely make a man more intriguing. And you know he'll have great pad to take you back to.

Me: What if a guy doesn't have money or power?

Lara: Then he has to be cool.

Meredith: Cool can even be sexier than rich.

Me: What makes a guy cool?

Lara: He knows the band that's playing. Or he's in a band. Or he's traveled all around the world and speaks at least one other language. Or he has a cool job like a record company exec or a journalist or a minor league baseball player.

Alyson: Or he could have a cool hobby like filmmaking, ice climbing, renovating old houses—something creative or intensely physical that he's really good at and enthusiastic about.

Carol: Having a dog is also sexy. Guys walking their dogs always catch my eye. You figure he must be caring and sweet if he can take care of a dog.

Lara: That's true. I always end up talking to the guy who's brought his dog to the bar.

Meredith: But cats are so unsexy.

Lara: Guys with cats are weird.

Me: Alyson, what do you think is sexy at first sight, before a guy has even opened his mouth?

Alyson: I love men who look a little slouchy, a little indie. Worn-in jeans, a paint-spattered T-shirt with an obscure logo on it. I love when a guy's hair is just a little too long and curls over his ears and at the back of his neck. Ooh, and I love it when tall, thin guys wear sweatshirts that are just a little too small for them.

Lara: And you can see a little of their back and stomach? That is so sexy.

Alyson: Oh, yeah.

Me: I like it when a guy wears a button-down shirt untucked under a wool sweater, so the tails come out at the bottom. It's schoolboy sexy.

Meredith: I know I said all that about power and money and stuff, but it does turn me on when a guy is a little boyish. Especially if he seems shy and sweet.

Lara: You know what's so sexy? If a guy rolls up the sleeves of his shirt or sweater and he has these really manly, muscular forearms.

Meredith: Hot. Very hot.

Alyson: I think it's sexy when a guy smiles a lot and just looks happy and relaxed. Oh, there is this one other thing. I'll check out what a guy is reading, and if it's by a great author—like Michael Chabon, not Tom Clancy— I absolutely adore that.

Lara: I go for the book thing, too. It's like nerd hot. You feel like he'll be incredible in bed because he's literary and therefore sensitive and emotionally intelligent.

Carol: This is such an explicit thing, I can't believe I'm saying it, but I like it when a guy is sitting across from you with his legs spread and you can kind of see the bulge in his jeans. Not like he has a hard-on or anything, but his package is just right there.

Meredith: I know what you mean. But it can't be because his pants are too tight. It's just like his package is big and there's nothing he can do about that. Thin denim gives the best view.

Me: It's like the equivalent of women having cleavage.

Alyson: And worn-out jeans are like the push-up bra.

Carol: Exactly.

3

THE
FIRST DATE

The Right Time and Place ■
Rocking the Date ■ Getting Physical

I've never gone on a second date with a guy I didn't end up in some kind of a relationship with. That's because it usually takes only one date (maybe two) for me to know we click—that is, we get each other's jokes, are physically attracted to each other, have plenty to talk about. And that's just the beginning.

When it comes to determining criteria for "clicking," women are extremely, almost maniacally, picky. We check out everything—from the way a guy smells to the way he walks, from what his hands look like to the kind of shoes he wears, from how often he shaves to the amount of jewelry he wears (the less the better). We even try to see if there's chemistry after only 5 minutes of conversation.

If you pass our initial evaluation, we start to notice other things about you, like your vocabulary, the way you treat a waitress, what you order off of the menu, whether or not you say "Cheers!" before taking a sip of your drink. The list goes on and on.

How do you survive this kind of scrutiny and come out on top? In spite of what you're up against, my best advice is this: Relax. Not just because you'll have a better time if you cop a Zen attitude about it all, but because women can't resist a relaxed man, regardless of how many criteria he meets. We think that if you're so chill, it must be because you're happy with who you are, successful with women, and basically a guy who has his life together. So hit the gym, take a long shower, chug a beer, then show up at her door with a warm smile that says simply, "Hey."

■ The Right Time and Place

My schedule is always packed with after-work meetings, pickup basketball games, parties, you name it. So when I meet a woman, I always face the same dilemma: Ask her out for 2 weeks later, or wait until the week I'm free?

Don't wait. Call her 1 or 2 days after you meet and explain that you're extremely busy for the next 2 weeks but you really want to see her. She'll probably be intrigued by the fact that you've clearly got a lot going on. I was.

What's the best night of the week to go on a date? Does it matter?

Ugh, it matters more than you could ever imagine. Women assume all sorts of things depending on what night you try to book us.

Here's the drill: Friday and Saturday nights are best—they're considered social prime time. If you take us out then, it means you're pretty interested. Which is good.

Percentage of singles ages 25 to 34 who report zero first dates in the past year: **40**

(SOURCE: match.com)

Thursdays are perfect if you want to send the message that you're very casual about the whole thing, or you're already busy on both weekend nights—a great strategy to use on women who acted as if they were doing you an honor just by giving you their digits. Sunday afternoons are a smart choice if you think a woman is afraid that you just want to sleep with her.

Mondays, Tuesdays, and Wednesdays? Don't even think about it, unless something really special—a must-see concert, sports event, play—is happening that night and that night only.

Do you always expect the guy to plan a date, or would you rather he ask for your input?

I don't necessarily expect a guy to pick a first-date destination, but I definitely prefer him to present some options. It assures me that he isn't one of those "I don't know, what do you want to do?" types (I hate that!), and it clues me in to what his tastes might be. I especially like it when a guy precedes his idea with a teaser. For example, if he asked, "Do you like Mexican food?" and I said yes, then he'd suggest a brand-new restaurant with a live mariachi band. Of course, if I hated rice and beans, he'd need a backup idea. Which leads me to my next tip: Always have a plan B and C.

Oh, and if you call a girl to ask her out and she already has a place picked out, it means that she's been thinking about you and is thrilled you called.

Do women consider dinner and a movie to be a lame first date?

I wouldn't call it lame, just predictable—we're always impressed if you can come up with something a little more creative.

Don't get me wrong. Dinner and a movie *can* be a good thing. You check each other out over wine and pasta, and then the pressure is off because you spend 2 hours focusing on something else. After the flick, you swap opinions over a drink or coffee, go for a walk, or just call it a night because by then it's already 1:00 A.M. You're never left feeling awkward or wondering what to do next.

Besides, being taken to a nice restaurant makes a woman feel like she's being treated special, which is really what we look for from a first date anyway.

> Percentage of female Penn State students who think "dinner and movie/getting coffee" is an ideal first date: **78**
>
> (SOURCE: Independent Woman's Club Penn State Dating Survey at shethinks.org)

Is it true that romantic comedies are the most appropriate movies for a first date? I just can't stand anything with Meg Ryan or Julia Roberts in it.

I've never understood why people think romantic comedies are good date movies. My friends and I always talk about how romantic comedies make downright *sucky* date movies. There you are with this guy you're trying to get to know, flirt with, and possibly seduce, and there's a couple on screen doing the exact same thing, only they're a lot better-looking. Intense action, horror, and suspense flicks top our list of date movie choices. They raise your body temperature and get your blood pumping, and you both leave the theater feeling physically restless. Perfect.

Oh, P.S.: Most women feel really uncomfortable if there's a lot of sex/nudity in a first-date flick (the only boobs she wants you to think about are hers). So scan reviews for T&A warnings.

I was thinking of asking this girl I just met to go bowling. Good idea?

Um . . . only if you know she likes to bowl. And, even then, if she's the tiniest bit high maintenance (does she wear high heels?), I'd save it for the third or fourth date, when the stakes aren't quite as high. The smelly saddle shoes, the merciless fluorescent lights, the startlingly high odds she'll slip and fall on her butt—you're just asking for trouble.

What's the best kind of restaurant to hit on a first date?

Take her to the swankest restaurant you've been to before and really liked. Everything you do will appear smooth because you already know what to expect, where to park, and what's good on the menu and wine list. Afterward, take her to a bar or lounge where you know you'll be able to find a romantic spot to sit, or take her for a walk through a pretty neighborhood. Bonus tip: If you do suggest going for a walk, be sure to ask if she's wearing comfortable shoes. We love that kind of consideration.

I'm going out with a woman who makes more money than I do. A lot more. I don't want her to think I'm cheap, but I can't afford

to take her to the kind of places she must be used to. What should I do?

Forget expensive or exclusive—just shoot for hip. Take her someplace that's "in" because a live jazz band plays during dinner, it's a little-known place in the middle of Chinatown, or they make the best damn brick-oven pizza in town. Besides, I'm sure this woman knows you're not in her tax bracket (women pick up on that stuff pretty fast), and if she's agreed to go out with you, she obviously doesn't mind.

■ Rocking the Date

How does a guy impress you on a first date? When is he trying too hard?

A guy is trying too hard if he pretends to be something he's not for my sake—like claiming he likes a band or author I mention when he's never really heard of them, or taking me to an expensive and trendy restaurant when in actuality he can't stand pretentious places.

When I go on a first date, I give the guy I'm with all of my attention. So what impresses me most is when he does the same (that means plenty of eye contact, listening carefully to what I'm saying, noticing when my drink is empty, et cetera). Anything less and I'll assume that by month four he'll be answering his cell phone during dates and falling asleep before I've had my orgasm.

The most impressive combo? When a guy is confident enough to be himself and sweet enough to stay focused on me.

How can I ace the first date?

Show up on time. Give her 100 percent of your attention all night long. Ask her interesting but lighthearted questions about who she is and what she likes. Respond openly when she asks you the same. Make her laugh. Give her sincere and intelligent compliments. Hold doors open for her. Pay the bill. Kiss her at the end of the night. Call the next day to say you had a great time.

Do all of the above and you're guaranteed at least a B+.

You mentioned that how you treat a waitress matters to the woman you're on a date with. Why? How should I treat her?

Percentage of women who want to be romanced and admit that having doors held open is an important part of that: **67**

(SOURCE: about.com poll)

Simple: Be polite and friendly, but not overattentive. And don't get mad if she screws up your order (but do say *something*—otherwise we'll think you're a pushover).

You see, any other behavior screams, "Jerk!" If you flirt with the waitress, say, or check out her bod—or do the same to any other woman under the age of 60, for that matter—we'll get the impression you're the womanizing type and be immediately turned off. And if you're rude to her, we'll think you're thoughtless and/or a snob.

What's the final word on who should pay the bill?

You offer to pay. Period.

Some women will protest and offer to split the check, but you should insist. Then smile, say you appreciate her offer, and that she can treat next time around.

What can a guy tell a girl about himself that will really spark her interest?

Anything that suggests you do fun things all the time, have direction in life, have good taste, aren't afraid to voice your opinion, have been to cool places, et cetera.

Some samples to work with: You just changed jobs because another company made an offer you couldn't refuse, you play piano, you have an awesome view from your office window, you taught English as a second language in Tibet, you were just hired to redesign J. Lo's official Web site, you scored two tickets to see The Hives next weekend, you blame American and European drug addicts for the war in Colombia, you've done incredibly well as a freelancer, you leave work early on Fridays for weekend bike trips, you're reading the novel just reviewed by the *New Yorker* and have something different to say about it, you adore your niece/nephew, you once built a ship, you listen to NPR, you yodel. . . .

What can you do if you're in the middle of a dud date and it's getting awkward because the conversation is dragging?

Order two martinis.

If that isn't an option, ask her some questions guaranteed to spark a lighthearted debate. One great strategy is to pose a game of ethics. Present this scenario to her: "You see a train hurtling down a track. If it continues on its current course, it will kill five people. If you pull a lever, it will change tracks and kill only one person. Do you pull the lever?" When she's answered that one, ask her: "What if the same train were about to plow down five people and you could stop it from reaching them by pushing one man—a stranger to you—in front of the train? Would you do it?"

That should make things interesting at least for a little while. It helps if you have a cache of conversation boosters like that to whip out as needed, so keep your eyes and ears peeled.

According to a survey of 220 women in *Men's Health* magazine, some restaurant orders win you points, while others label you a loser.
Dishes that say . . .
"Confident" or "Keeper"
Filet mignon
Burgers and fries
Jambalaya
Lobster and steak
"Dull" or "Strapped for cash"
Chicken with rice
Pasta primavera
Pork loin and potatoes
Chicken Caesar salad

I'm being set up with a woman who has a 10-year-old son. Any advice? Should I get her to talk about him, or avoid the subject altogether?

Rule of thumb when dating gals with kids: Single moms don't want to feel like single moms when they're on a date. So when you're out with her, ask about her son so she knows you're interested in him, but don't linger on the topic too long. Otherwise, simply treat her as you would any other attractive, available woman. Just don't act impatient or disappointed when she calls it a night at 11:00 P.M. because the babysitter has a curfew. It'll prove you understand and respect her responsibilities.

Percentage of online daters who are open to dating someone with children: **74**

(SOURCE: match.com)

What's the appropriate move after a great date? Should I send flowers? Call her? Wait for her to call me?

If you really like her, you should call her the next afternoon to let her know you had a good time. If it was an epic first date—you stayed up all night Rolfing, got the same tattoo, became blood brothers, or if you're truly head over heels for her already—you could send flowers. Otherwise it will seem a little dramatic and eager to please. If you have a feeling this girl is trying to play hard to get with you, wait until 2 days (but no longer than 2 days) after, just to beat her at her own game.

■ Getting Physical

What moves can you make during a date to let a woman know you're physically attracted to her and find out if she feels the same?

Sit so your legs touch hers. If she doesn't move away, that's a good sign. If you want to take it up a notch, rest your hand lightly on her knee during conversation and leave it there for a few minutes. If she squirms or looks uncomfortable, she wants you to back off. If she pretends not to notice but keeps smiling and talking, it means she likes the physical attention. If you want to be even more forward, reach for her hand or stroke her forearm. Again, look for a positive response—smiling, leaning toward you, touching you back—to clue you in that she's hot for you, too.

What makes a really great first kiss?

The ultimate first kisses are always a little overdue. So, if you can, wait until the sexual tension is so high it's distorting the air between you like gasoline fumes. Pick a quiet, cinematic spot: outside a cozy restaurant under the yellow glow of a streetlight, a little table in a mellow lounge, under a big tree during a postdinner stroll. Slide your arm around her waist, move toward her slowly, and make soft but decisive lip contact. In my opinion, a first kiss should always be a French one. It sends the message that you can't quite contain your attraction for her—she'll think that's so hot her knees will buckle.

Is there any way to make a first kiss even sexier?

Glad you asked. There's an area halfway between her armpit and hip on the sides of her torso that's a bit of a sweet spot. While you're kissing her, put your hands on her waist, then slide them up to this part of her body, just barely brushing the side of her breasts as you do it. You'll be turning her on without really making a move, which is perfect for a first- or second-date situation. There's something about that almost touch that makes us kind of crazy.

Percentage of women who agree that kissing on the first date is appropriate: **66**

Percentage of those women who say the kiss should come at the very end of the date: **45**

(SOURCE: Yahoo! Personals online survey)

Why do women usually refuse to sleep with guys on the first date?

Most of my friends have adopted a no-nookie-on-the-first-date policy for several reasons (the Surgeon General would be disappointed to learn that not one of them is health-related):

1. They don't want to seem slutty—to you or to themselves.
2. They're afraid you won't consider them the "girlfriend type" (because you'll think they're slutty), and therefore will respond with a booty call instead of an invitation for a second date.
3. They want to find out if you think they're worth waiting for.

4. They like the romance of moving slowly and savoring each elevation in physical affection, so that by the time you do have sex, it feels truly climactic.

The good news? It's usually not because we don't want to.

I don't feel comfortable swapping body fluids with someone I've hung out with only once. If a woman asks me to spend the night after a first date, what's the nicest way to turn her down?

Tell her you want to wait because you like her so much you don't want to risk going too fast. She'll be a little embarrassed and feel rejected . . . so follow your refusal with a nice long kiss.

After you're gone, she'll call up her best friend to tell her what happened. Together they'll wonder what your deal is. Were you just not attracted to her? Did you write her off as a bimbo the minute she invited you in? Or maybe you have some strange physical deformity you're afraid to reveal (like a penis the size of a pea pod).

It certainly won't stop her from going on a second or a third date with you   it'll just keep her guessing.

If you have sex with someone on the first date, is it rude to not stay over?

Not as long as you're extremely romantic about making your exit. Remember, she barely knows you herself and isn't necessarily looking forward to waking up next to you all crusty-eyed and groggy.

The best strategy is, after cuddling for a minimum of an hour (yes, an entire hour), tell her you want to head home so you're not in her way come sunrise. If she insists you stay, and sounds hurt that you even contemplated leaving, you probably should sack out for the night. Otherwise, give her some heartfelt hugs and kisses and tell her you'll call tomorrow at 11:00 A.M. (giving an exact time will assure her you mean it—and you do, right?). She'll lie in bed feeling all tingly and excited about what just happened and will be psyched to hear from you again.

GIRLS OVERHEARD:
Sex on the First Date

The Scene

My favorite Irish bar after work on a Thursday night. We're tucked away at a corner table, drinking pints and trying not to be overheard by the two 60-year-old men sitting next to us.

The Guest List

Celia, 28, a magazine editor
Courtney, 26, a computer programmer
Stephanie, 30, a grant writer and musician
Eileen, 21, a film major and part-time bartender

Me: How often do you guys sleep with a guy the first time you go out with him?

Courtney: An official date, right? Not just a one-night wonder you met at a party?

Me: Right. You agree to go out, have dinner, a movie, whatever.

Courtney: I've done it a couple of times. I don't think women do it all that much, though.

Celia: I have, too. You end up back at your apartment at the end of the date and one thing leads to another and no one says, "We should stop," so you don't.

Eileen: But is a guy ever going to be the one to say it?

Stephanie: Highly unlikely.

Me: So what made you decide to invite the guy back to your place?

Courtney: He drove me home and walked me to the door and we started kissing and it was out of this world. He kissed me so intensely, my legs melted. I knew he was going to be incredible in bed. So I just unlocked my front door and held it open for him and he walked in. We didn't even discuss it.

Celia: You must have been awfully horny that day.

Courtney: I was. The fact that I hadn't had sex for a year before going on that date probably had something to do with it, but I wasn't desperate by any means. It was like I was starving and someone just happened to put a filet mignon in front of me. I wouldn't have gone for it if it were just ground beef. Ugh, sorry about the meat metaphors.

Me: But what happened on the date that made you so hot for this guy?

Courtney: We went to a very sexy, dimly lit little restaurant for dinner, and then we went to a bar with live jazz for a nightcap. We had so much in common, we talked each other's ears off. It just felt right. By 11:00 P.M. we were sitting really close to each other with his arm around me and my hand on his knee.

Stephanie: I can't relate. I've never had sex on a first date. I feel like it completely ruins the romance and anticipation of the whole dating thing. Making a guy wait for sex—and making yourself wait, too—shows you're serious about wanting a meaningful relationship, not just a fling. Besides, I just can't deal with getting naked and sweaty with a total stranger.

Eileen: I agree that sleeping together too soon can screw things up. I slept with a guy on the first date after we had gone out dancing at a club, and by the third week of dating and having sex, things just fell apart. I didn't trust the guy yet. I didn't know what else was going on in his life. We only spoke to each other every few days, but we were already taking showers together. It felt really weird, and neither of us knew how to act with the other. It's one thing if you're just screwing and that's it. That's crystal clear. But trying to start a relationship that way can get confusing.

Celia: Granted, sometimes it's a mistake. But one of the times that I did it on a first date was with my ex who I ended up dating for 2 years. On our first date we had been talking about how he built a funky bench out of two old snowboards, so as we were leaving the bar, he asked if I wanted to go check it out. I honestly went to his apartment to see the bench, I swear. But then he whipped up some great sour apple martinis and played some old Rolling Stones records and we started talking and kissing and one thing led to another. We ended up having the hottest sex that night. But I definitely felt weird about it the next day and told him I was afraid things had moved way too fast. But the sex never got in the way—it just kept getting better.

Me: What if the sex wasn't good? Do you think you would have ended up going out again?

Celia: Wow, I don't know. Probably not. Things are so fragile on a first date that bad sex would make a second date incredibly awkward.

Courtney: A first date that involves dancing and drinking is about 50 times more likely to end up in bed than a quiet date where you go to the movies or something.

Stephanie: Well, if you're grinding up against each other, you're already halfway there.

Eileen: Wait a second, about that bad-sex point—first-date sex is super risky, not just because of the obvious health and safety reasons but because you're so damn critical of someone the first few times you hang out with them. I mean, if you've started falling for someone over the past month and you find out he has a hairy back, you're probably not going to be turned off by it because you sincerely like him. But after just one superficial night, a hairy back might be enough to make you write a guy off.

Celia: I have a confession to make. Last year I went on a date with this incredible guy, Alex. He worked for an environmental law firm, rode a motorcycle, and looked like Benicio Del Toro. I was blown away. At the end of the date I could tell I was more impressed with him than he was with me, so I decided to take him back to my place and show him a few of my hidden talents. I just wanted him to know what he'd be missing if we didn't go out again.

Courtney: Did he ask you out again after that?

Celia: Oh, yeah. But it didn't last. His company transferred him to California.

Stephanie: So you weren't sure if he was crazy about you and you used sex to boost his interest. I guess as long as you knew what you were doing and didn't care, it's your prerogative. Nobody got hurt.

Celia: I also wasn't looking for a serious relationship. I just wanted to fool around for a little while. Most women don't want that.

Me: You're hardly a freak. Plenty of women like having a bed buddy between boyfriends.

Eileen: Right. So if you sleep with a guy on the first date, he'll think of you as a bed buddy, not as a potential girlfriend.

Stephanie: He might. That's a risk. I'm sure a lot of women don't sleep with a guy right away because they don't want him to think they're easy.

Courtney: Oh, definitely. We all learned that lesson in high school.

Me: So what do you do if you're dying to sleep with a guy who you've only just met?

Courtney: Wait until the fourth or fifth date.

Eileen: Or at least the second.

4

SORT OF SEEING EACH OTHER

Make Her Crazy for You ■ **First-Time Sex** ■ **Her Most Confusing Moves** ■ **Casual-Dating Dilemmas**

By now you've gone out a few times, and—as far as you know—everything is going well (she still takes your calls, right?), but you wouldn't exactly call her your "girlfriend." Welcome to the state of total dating ambiguity known among my friends as "sort of seeing each other."

The perk: a backstage pass to a brand-new female body and mind. The problem: you have no idea what's actually back there.

This roller coaster of a mutual trial period makes the bar scene seem like a slow drive in the country. After every date, you'll both be wondering—and worrying—about where you stand and whether you're right for each other. And the chance that either of you will make a sound judgment while in the throes of new-relationship lust? Pretty darn slim. Inevitably, this carnival ride will end with The Talk—during which you either decide to call yourselves a couple or call other prospects.

It's no surprise to me that I have an inbox full of questions related to this limbo period. So here's my advice on all things "sort of"—

first-time sex, keeping her interested, casual-dating dilemmas, long-distance dating, and much more.

■ Make Her Crazy for You

Does it pay to play hard to get with a girl? How can I do it right?

A certain type of girl likes this challenge—but usually because she has a self-esteem problem. So, for example, if a guy is totally into her, she'll think something is wrong with him. Conversely, if a guy ignores her, she'll think something is wrong with her—and the only way to prove otherwise is to get his approval. In this game, it's not really you she's interested in; she just wants to validate her own desirability. So does it pay? You decide.

Now, how to reel her in. Don't approach her, but when she finally approaches you, act like you've been waiting all night to talk to her. When you're with her, treat her like gold. When you're not with her, don't call or e-mail. Wait for her to call you. When she does, call her back right away. These mixed signals will drive a game-playing girl insane—and make her determined to win you over.

I've just started dating this amazing woman. She's smart, beautiful, fun, sexy. What can I do to keep her as interested in me as I am in her?

Two things: First, let her know what you're good at. For all the talk about women being wowed by money and power, intelligence and ability are just as sexy (in fact, sexier to any woman with self-respect). So go ahead, show off your skills. Have you been playing the guitar since you were 7? Do you speak French and Spanish? Did you learn how to salsa on your last trip to Cuba? Do you make a killer dirty martini?

Second, make her feel special. The man who seems most like Prince Charming is the one who makes me

> Research has shown that people dating someone new have brain patterns similar to those of people suffering from obsessive-compulsive disorder.
>
> (SOURCE: *Psychological Medicine*, 1999, Volume 29)

feel most like a princess. So open doors for her, listen closely to what she has to say, consider her feelings, compliment her often. Let her know she blows you away just by being herself.

Got any original date ideas?

1. Rent your favorite Woody Allen movie and grill hot dogs on your fire escape.
2. Get tickets to the opera even though neither of you knows jack about it.
3. Go to a bright, cheery bar on a Saturday afternoon. Get trashed.
4. Borrow a friend's dog and try to teach it new tricks.
5. Go see a bad heavy-metal band in concert. Make fun of the crowd.
6. Eat dinner at a rooftop restaurant with a phat view (hotels often have 'em).
7. Play Frisbee golf in the park. Rules: Pick a tree in the distance. See who can hit it in the fewest throws. Equipment: two Frisbees, one big open field.
8. Watch a Little League Baseball game. Cheer for the runts.
9. Find an air hockey table and play for money.
10. Go dancing someplace where you're the only two people not retired.

I just started dating a woman 2 weeks ago and I'm totally confused about what I should do for Valentine's Day. Any suggestions?

Yes: Hand-deliver a small surprise to her office with a note (*not* a Hallmark card) from you saying "Happy V-Day." A new boyfriend did that for me once and I loved it. A dozen roses is too touchy-feely, not to mention cliché, for such a new relationship, so think of something small that's either funny or edible. Maybe she mentioned that she's a closet Neil Diamond fan. If so, get her a CD with the cheesiest cover shot of Neil you can find. Did she confess to a weakness for cinnamon buns? Leave a jumbo one in a box with her name on it. Do you know her favorite order at

HOME BASE Does Your Pad Add Up?

From a woman's point of view, what you put in your pad either adds to your allure or damages your image. Where do you stand? Grab a pencil and do the math. (Score a zero next to items you don't have.)

Your pad has ...	Point value	Points scored
Original art	+10	_____
Self-portrait	–6	_____
Wineglasses	+7	_____
Shot glasses from all 50 states	–10	_____
Nice area rug	+6	_____
Wall-to-wall carpet	–4	_____
Family pictures	+12	_____
Celebrity posters	–15	_____
Books stacked on your bedroom floor	+8	_____
Magazines stacked on your bathroom floor	–8	_____
High-powered laptop	+9	_____
3-year-old PC	–8	_____

Starbucks? Buy her a chai latte skim (or whatever it is) and have the receptionist call up to let her know there's something hot waiting for her in the lobby. She'll be surprised and flattered in just the right amounts.

My apartment is a mess—milk crates, bike parts, yellowed newspapers, dirty plates, the bathroom has never been cleaned. What's the minimum I can do to make my pad presentable to a new girlfriend?

Halogen lamp	−10	_____
Down comforter	+10	_____
Empty fridge	−4	_____
Quality pots and pans	+8	_____
Fireplace	+9	_____
Milk crates as furniture	−10	_____
Dog	+20	_____
Cat	−10	_____
Two cats	−15	_____
	Total score:	_____

What your score means:

60+ You dazzled.

30 to 60 You made a good impression.

0 to 30 Neutral.

0 to −30 We forgive if you're otherwise great.

−30 to −60 We describe your bad taste to our friends and will likely call off our next date.

−60 to −100 Um, gotta go!

First, your toilet, sink, and shower *must* be clean. Pay to have it done once if necessary. Second, clear surfaces are everything. It's better to pile neat stacks of papers, magazines, or mail on the floor than to have them jumbled on top of the TV, coffee table, kitchen counters, et cetera. Third, wash your sheets! (A made-up bed won't hurt either.) Beyond those basics, light a few candles in your otherwise dark bedroom before taking her in there and she won't notice or care about the pile of dirty laundry festering in the corner—and by morning, it won't matter as much.

I've been on three dates with an ad exec and things are going well. Except . . . I think she's turned off by the fact that I'm in construction (when we met, jobs didn't come up until after we'd flirted for 2 hours). How can I make her ditch her blue-collar aversion?

I'm not surprised she has this prejudice, and I'm sure you're not either. It's no secret that women judge men by their jobs the way men judge women by their looks. The best thing in this case is show her you don't need a college education to be intelligent, or a high-powered job to be a confident, funny, thoughtful, and an otherwise all-around amazing guy. If she agrees to go on dates four and five with you, she's obviously willing to look past the fact that you're not the VIP she'd always imagined herself with.

I met this great girl on a snowboarding trip, but she lives three states away. We want to try the long-distance thing. Any advice on how to keep her interested from afar?

Shower her with affection to make up for the fact that you're not actually around. So . . . send her an e-mail or call her at least once every other day. Send her something cute in the mail—like a mixed CD or a book you think she'd like. More important, plan a weekend together ASAP. Wait too long before you see each other again and her memory of you in the flesh will fade. Do it for your own sake, too. Until you see what she's like on her home turf, you won't really know this girl.

Percentage of women who postponed sex in their "best relationship yet" until . . .

The first date: **9**
The second to fourth dates: **26**
The fifth to ninth dates: **22**
The tenth date or later: **17**
Percentage of them who say they are waiting for marriage: **26**

(SOURCE: about.com Dating Survey)

■ First-Time Sex

What does a woman expect the first time you have sex?

We expect that it'll be a little clumsy at first, then frantic and passionate, then over very, very fast.

It doesn't take that many first encounters to realize that few men can restrain themselves from coming for

long when they're inside someone new. As for us, we don't expect to come at all (unless maybe we get lucky and the novelty
of it all sends us over the edge even before you get there).

All of which doesn't make it any less exhilarating. We're
intoxicated the moment we feel you through your pants
and realize we're going to have this forbidden part of you in
the palm of our hand and then other wetter, warmer places.
It's all so erotic it doesn't take much at all to make this night
exceptional.

We were hammered the first time we had sex. Now she's afraid that having sex again would be rushing things. Please explain this logic to me.

It's complicated, but here's the abbreviated version: She feels like
she messed up and wants to fix it. The thing is, she probably
really likes you. And when we really like a guy, we want the relationship to progress slowly, the way traditional, romantic, healthy
relationships should. She's likely afraid that sleeping together too
soon screws up a relationship, so now she wants to pretend it
didn't happen in the first place. It's a little silly, I know.

You don't have much of a choice other than to respect her
wishes. And my advice is to not make a big deal about it—you'll
be in the sack again in no time.

I have genital herpes. The girl I've been dating doesn't know, but we haven't had sex yet either. How and when is the best time to tell her?

You have to tell her before you
have sex with her, but you
should wait as long as possible.
Every fun date you go on will
increase the chances that she
won't consider your STD a deal
breaker. She may be mad that
you waited, but it's better than

Percentage of people in the
United States infected with
an STD: **20**

Percentage of all STD cases that
occur in people 25 years old or
younger: **66**

Percentage of adults who would
be less likely to continue a relationship if they found out their
date had an STD: **60**

(SOURCES: The American Social Health Association; Roper Starch Worldwide Survey)

telling her too soon and having her write you off before she even gets to know you.

How can I let a woman I'm sleeping with for the first time know I'm experienced and good in bed, without freaking her out with too much too soon?

That's easy: Just do the basic things extra well, and throw in a few not-so-basic things to show her you're more creative than the average guy. For example, don't just kiss her nipples; swirl your tongue around them as if they were soft-serve ice cream cones. Plant kisses up the entire length of her spine. Stroke her thighs while thrusting into her. Take breaks to kiss her and rub her clitoris at the same time. Your finesse will impress her more than any kinky parlor tricks.

RUBBER MATCH Judging a Boy by His Cover

Which condom you wear the first time you have sex with a woman makes a difference. Here's what we're thinking when your willy is wearing something . . .

Colored: You're too funny. No, really. You're actually being too funny. Making love for the first time is supposed to be romantic, not a barrel of laughs, and a colored condom is pretty much a joke.

Name-brand and basic: Like Levi's, a no-frills condom by a reputable manufacturer always looks and feels right. We'll assume you're concerned with safety (but not overly) and you won't try anything kinky before we're ready.

Textured: You're probably experienced and like to get the most possible pleasure out of every erotic encounter. We'll think you're more likely than most guys to try something wild. Some women will be intimidated, others thrilled.

I know it's difficult for some women to orgasm, but how can I increase the chance she'll have one the first time I'm with her?

The formula for female orgasm is complicated and always a little different from one woman to the next. Add to that the pressures of first-time sex and you have a formula for disappointment. One way to increase her odds is to take things slow from the start so she can get completely aroused before intercourse.

As I'm sure you know, most women need lots of steady clitoral stimulation to have an orgasm. The best strategy: During intercourse, rub her clitoris and the surrounding area with the pads of your index, middle, and ring fingers held together, increasing in speed and pressure as she gets more excited. You can also encourage her to get on top—the most popular orgasm-producing position for women. Or go down on her and

All-natural: Animal-derived condoms gross us out because we can't deal with the fact that part of a dead sheep has landed in our privates. If you like that idea, you're not the kind of guy we want to date. (Plus, this is the only kind of condom that doesn't protect against HIV and hepatitis B, so we still wouldn't use it.)

Spermicidal: You're sexually conservative and extremely cautious. Spermicide smells funky and can cause health problems for some women, so it may not be worth the extra safety. The fact that you opt in means you might be a little too concerned. Then again, a more conservative woman might see that as positive.

Generic/economy: You're cheap and don't pay attention to detail. If you're looking to save a buck on sex, we sure don't want you around come birthday time.

The use of condoms, especially when having sex for the first time, may lead to closer, more intimate, and longer-lasting relationships.

(SOURCE: University of Georgia)

alternate stimulating her clitoris with your fingers and tongue. Sliding a finger into her vagina and pumping the area on the front wall of her vagina to stimulate the G-spot while you lick her clitoris can also have orgasmic results.

If, in spite of your efforts, she doesn't hit her high, don't worry about it. We never expect a guy to get it right away, so don't go overboard trying to get her there the first time around (if you do and she can't make it happen, she'll feel inadequate and embarrassed—or she'll fake it to satisfy you, which doesn't help either of you). Instead, show her how great you are in bed by lavishing attention on every inch of her body. Bonus tip: Saying something like "I can't wait to learn how to make you come" will assure her you haven't given up on her.

Is it really necessary to have a birth-control conversation? Can't I just reach for a condom at the appropriate moment?

I called up a few of my friends and they agree that it's okay just to pull out a condom. Although my friend Sarah suggests showing her the condom and saying, "Is this okay or is there something else you'd rather use?"

I never know what to say to a woman after the first time we have sex. What would she want me to say?

1. "You are so beautiful."
2. "That was amazing."
3. "You're wonderful."

■ Her Most Confusing Moves

Why do women you've just started dating want to know so much about past relationships? I don't want to reveal anything that might ruin my chances with her.

Chalk up most of our questions to self-preservation or simple curiosity. We ask about your ex-girlfriends because we want to know who else you've been attracted to, who we're being compared with, and whether there's a long-lost love who might resurface and steal you away. We ask about your breakups because we want to avoid making the same mistakes. We ask about your sex life because we want to know how experienced you are.

This doesn't mean we're ready for the answers—so you're right to be cautious about what you spill. In fact, full disclosure is unnecessary and a bad idea. Just be honest, but in the most conservative way possible. Juicy little tidbits of info, like your college girlfriend paid her tuition by modeling swimsuits or you had your first threesome at age 27—which was just 6 months ago—don't do anyone any good.

Why don't women call guys after a date? I've gone on four dates with this woman and I'm always the one who does the postdate calling.

When we don't call you, it's because we want you to call us. After every date, we wonder if you're still interested, and that phone call reassures us.

At least that applies to the first and second dates. By the third, most women will feel comfortable enough to call you. The fact that this chick is phone shy may mean she just needs more reassurance than most of us. Either that or she's playing games—making you pursue her so she'll feel more desirable. Either way, the best thing is just to call her. When she finally realizes you're sincerely interested, she'll quit this not-calling crap.

Percentage of women who say they'll call a guy after a first date instead of waiting for him to call: **71**

(SOURCE: *American Demographics* magazine, February 2002)

I don't get it—when we go out, we have a great time. She just doesn't seem crazy about me. Like when I call or e-mail her, she

usually takes a couple of days to respond, and then she doesn't seem that into it. What's going on here?

I think you're right. She likes you but, as you say, isn't crazy about you. When a woman starts dating a guy she's nuts about, she can barely contain herself. Even if she's trying to force herself to take things slow, she won't be able to wait longer than 24 hours to return your call or e-mail. And since she hasn't wanted to take the physical part beyond kissing, she clearly isn't consumed by lust. Her interest in you may grow as you continue to date, but my hunch is she dates you because she likes you—while she holds out for that certain someone else. Keep dating her if you enjoy her company, but keep your eyes open for other opportunities.

We've gone on five fantastic dates. It's crystal clear that she's attracted to me, but if I suggest anything more than a kiss at the end of a date, she shuts me down. What's up with her?

Plenty of women I know wait until the tenth date or later before hitting the sheets. If she really seems psyched to go out with you (you say the dates are fantastic) but just isn't putting out, it could be because she takes the physical part of a relationship very seriously and prefers to wait until she really knows someone before getting intimate—which is pretty common. And it's not because she's a prude; she's just being careful with her emotions and her body.

A woman I work with has invited me out for drinks a few times. When I show up, she's always with a group of friends. Are these dates?

Nope.

That said, she may want a date with you and is just waiting for *you* to ask. If she spends the majority of each group outing talking and flirting with you and you alone, that's probably the case. Otherwise, she's just a socialite who likes bringing people together—maybe you should start checking out her friends.

How can you tell if a girl you've just started dating is seeing other guys at the same time?

Short of asking her point-blank, your only option is to look for subtle signs that you're not the only man in her life. Here are a few: She usually has "something else to do" on one weekend night. She won't listen to her answering machine when you're within earshot. She hasn't slept with you yet, and doesn't seem like she will anytime soon. She excuses herself to take a cell phone call during a date with you. She doesn't recognize your voice when you call. If you are having sex, more condoms have disappeared from the box in her bedside table than you can account for. Of course, there could be other explanations for all of these things—that's why, if you really want to know, you should just ask.

HIDDEN MEANING Five Subtle Signs She's into You

1. **Her voice always sounds upbeat when you call.** Women are moody, but a call from a guy we're interested in will squelch our inner bitch in a heartbeat.
2. **She's heard some news about something you're into.** If you've mentioned you like black-and-white photography and she brings up a Stieglitz exhibit, she wants to impress you.
3. **The bottom of her high heels are scuff-free.** Buying new shoes is our way of beating our chests. We want you to think we're hot.
4. **She laughs a little too much.** She's nervous because she likes you so much.
5. **She sends flawless e-mails.** If she never misspells a word and responds to your every question/comment, it's because she reads your e-mails at least three times before hitting send, and double-checks her own so she'll seem as smart/funny/clever as possible.

Overall, this girl I've gone out with five or six times doesn't seem all that intelligent, and conversations with her can be boring. But every once in a while, she'll say something so insightful and interesting I'll be blown away. Should I keep dating her, waiting for those rare moments of genius?

Will those "rare moments" ever be enough to satisfy your need for intellectual stimulation? Do you really want to spend a lot of time with someone who's not "all that intelligent" and can be downright "boring"? No, man. The answer is no.

What are the big differences between what younger women and older women want/need in the beginning of a relationship?

At 21, a girl hasn't had the experience (a.k.a. wrenching heartbreak) that teaches her not to throw herself headlong into a relationship. So she wants/needs that level of attention (phone calls, e-mails, dates, sleepovers, compliments, up-all-night heart-to-hearts) from a guy right off the bat.

By 35, a woman has learned to be more careful with her emotions. So she tends to want less from a man she's just met. Two dates over the course of a week and maybe a couple of phone calls in between feel like enough until it's clear both people are interested in taking it further.

This girl who turns me down whenever I ask her out will sometimes call up all friendly and want to hang out on a weeknight. We never actually hook up. What's she up to?

Bad news, man: She's using you. She's never going to date you exclusively and she probably won't sleep with you either. This chick just wants to know you're hanging on for that random Tuesday night when the guy she's really after is ignoring her and she needs to feel attractive and popular.

Certain girls (specifically, those who need constant attention from guys to feel good about themselves) do this all the time. They like having a fan club to fall back on. It's very lame behavior. Unless you want to keep her around simply for amusement yourself, claim you have another date the next time she requests a last-minute get-together.

I've dated many women who insist they don't want a serious relationship, then after 3 months of dating they want to have The Talk. Do any women mean it when they say they just want a casual fling?

Of course they do. The women who told you they weren't boyfriend hunting probably meant it as the words came out of their mouths. (Granted, they could have been lying to themselves, but that's different from lying to you.) Then, along the way, they got a little more attached to you than they expected. Be flattered that after dating you for just 3 months, several women decided that you were so great, they wanted more.

Given that you both agreed up front to keep things casual, no one could call you a jerk for not wanting to take things to the next level. She may feel rejected, but she can't say that you treated her unfairly.

■ Casual-Dating Dilemmas

When I'm in a new relationship, I'm not willing to let it get in the way of work, the gym, or hanging with my buds. That leaves time for just one date a week. How do I explain to a woman that, until I'm ready to get serious, that's all I'll invest?

Let her know before you go on your first date so she won't take it personally. She'll be flattered if you put it this way: "I don't have much time to date more than once a week these days because I've been incredibly busy. But you seem so great, I'd love to take you out anyway." If she asks why you're so busy all the time, blame it on work instead of saying you'd rather be hanging with the guys.

I tend to be too nice to women, and then it seems they just want me as a friend. I have no trouble meeting women and I do date, but we almost always end up "buddies." Why do nice guys finish last?

Because most single women out there aren't waiting for a nice guy to come along—we're waiting for sparks to fly. No sparks, and we keep looking.

While "nice" is definitely a quality we appreciate, it's not one that makes our palms sweat or our hearts beat faster or leaves us wanting more after every date. After all, on the first date a nice guy won't tell a woman she looks incredibly sexy even if he's thinking it; he won't make fun of the froufrou way she holds her cocktail glass; and he definitely won't put his hands on that sweet spot just above her hips when he kisses her good night. Maybe you're trying so hard to be, um, nice that you're not really being yourself.

What I'm getting at: If you want sparks, you have to make friction—and that means taking risks. Next time you feel you're coming across as merely benign, confess an unpopular opinion, tease her a little, give in to an urge to do something unexpected—and when you kiss her, do it like you don't give a damn if she thinks you're nice.

I've started fooling around with a female friend, but neither of us has acknowledged the change in our relationship. I want her to know I'd like to date her, but I don't want to screw things up (or stop fooling around even if she doesn't want to date me). What should I say?

Ooh, that's tricky. I'd wait awhile to see how her behavior changes before saying anything. If she seems to want to spend more time with you in person, on the phone, et cetera, she probably feels the same way you do. Go ahead and confess that you're into her in a boyfriend/girlfriend way.

If nothing else about the relationship changes other than the nighttime fondling, you risk freaking her out. Lie low until you can better gauge her feelings and enjoy the hookups while you wait.

If you're not sure where she stands and have to know how she feels *right now*, I guess you'll have to spill your guts. But if you lose out on the frisky fun, don't say I didn't warn you.

For the past six or seven dates, I've paid for everything and she's never offered to pick up the bill. Problem is, I'm not exactly rolling in it. How can I politely inform her that she has to start dropping some cash?

In high school I dated a guy who paid for everything—because he was 18 with a job, and I was 15 with an allowance. Unless you're the adult equivalent (read: a millionaire), she has no reason to expect you to foot the bill forever. But you knew that.

Here's what you do: Next time the bill comes, say, "Hey, would you mind splitting this with me? I'd love to treat you, but I've been living way over budget lately." If she's at all sensitive, she'll offer to pay and get the hint that you're no sugar daddy. Should she continue to pretend the check is invisible on future dates, just keep asking her to go dutch until she gets it.

I think my sort-of girlfriend is snooping when I leave her alone in my apartment. Should I confront her about it or what?

Listen, all women snoop a little when left alone in a man's apartment, whether it's just peeking into his medicine cabinet or opening a closet door to see if it's as messy as ours is. So if you've got something to hide, you might want to hide it better.

The good news is that because she's not supposed to be snooping, she can't confront you with anything she finds. Then again, if her foraging is more than just harmlessly curious—she's rifling through your desk, leaving letters and bills in disarray, or pulling stuff out from under your bed and making telltale tracks in the dust—you should confront her. She could be the insanely jealous type who will never respect your independence or privacy. (Just don't accuse her unless you're 99 percent sure, or *you'll* look like the psycho.)

I accidentally dropped the L-bomb during sex with my girlfriend of a few months. I'm pretty sure it doesn't really count during the deed, and she didn't say it back—but now I'm worried. I don't want her to get all clingy on me. Did my slipup take us to the next level? I love being with her, but I'm not ready to be that serious.

You're "pretty" sure it doesn't "really" count during the deed? I can see you have a lot of confidence in that theory. C'mon, you know it counts and you know it made an impact on her.

But you underemphasize a key piece of information here: She didn't say it back. Listen, if your girl were the clingy, get-her-claws-in-you type, wouldn't she have jumped at the chance to seal the deal with an enthusiastic "I love you, too!" She probably remained silent because, like you, she feels it's too soon.

You have two choices at this point. First, you could be a chump and pretend it never happened—but be forewarned: Couples that don't communicate openly are screwed for more reasons than I have room to list here. That's why you're better off addressing it directly. Just tell her what you told me (well, some of it, anyway). Say that you love being with her and you like the way things are going, but that you said something the other night without thinking. You just got a little ahead of yourself, is all, and want to save that particular statement for some time in the future when you feel 100 percent sure about it. She'll probably be relieved.

What's the best way to reschedule a date when you don't really have a good reason? Is it okay to lie and say something important came up?

Why not just explain it this way? Tell her you have something else you really want to do that you can't reschedule. Follow that immediately by saying you really want to see her soon, and can you make it up to her tomorrow night. At the beginning of a relationship, women usually are more easygoing about that kind of thing than you might think.

This girl I'm dating wants to talk about whether our relationship is going to get more serious. I don't see any point in having this talk yet because I'm just not sure about her. Is it possible to postpone the talk without freaking her out and making her cry?

I don't think it's possible to tell her you need more time without making her cry and freak out. (Sorry.) But you still need to tell her. (Sorry again.)

Soften the blow by explaining that you're really happy with the way things have been going so far; you're just not sure if you want to take it to the next level yet. Be reassuring, but don't make any promises. And definitely give her a big, warm hug when the tears start rolling.

Women's favorite comfort foods . . .
Ice cream: **74**
Chocolate: **69**
Cookies: **66**

(SOURCE: Brian Wansink, Ph.D., University of Illinois)

A girl I just started dating has a framed picture of her ex on a bookshelf. It's pretty dusty and stuck in a corner, but it bugs me. Can I ask her to get rid of it, or should I just toss it myself since she's probably forgotten it's there?

Since you've only just started seeing each other, no, you can't ask her to start redecorating her apartment (or do it for her). But next time she's in the room with you, you can point to the photo and ask about him to let her know you've noticed. If she gets a dreamy look in her eyes and says, "Oh, him? That's Bruce. He was this amazing surfer slash guitarist slash brain surgeon who moved to Australia," at least you know to keep an eye out in case Bruce comes back to town. If she says, "Ugh, I meant to throw that out months ago," and heaves it, then problem solved.

I want my new girlfriend and friends to get along, but the crowd I hang with looks something like the cast of *Animal House*. She's a suit-wearing, professional type who won't be amused

by their puke stories and immature sarcasm. How can I make her see that they're really worth getting to know?

Hmm. This might take some time. For best results, introduce her to each "animal" individually on different nights—and plan something that doesn't involve booze. That way your buds will be on their best behavior and more likely to make a good impression. Then warn her that the guys *can* get a little rowdy when they're all out together. (Which she probably expects from a group of guys, anyway.) Beyond that, you've just got to hope she has a good sense of humor and some faith that you wouldn't be friends with a bunch of morons if they didn't have something valuable—or at least fun—to offer.

GIRLS OVERHEARD:
How Often Do Women Think about Sex?

The Scene
Walking around New York City and shopping on a Saturday afternoon. We had most of this conversation while trying on clothes in a fitting room at Bloomingdale's.

The Guest List
Melissa, 30, a freelance financial reporter
Coco, 22, an acting student and waitress at a trendy restaurant
Danny, 26, an IT exec who works way too hard

Me: Guys have a reputation for thinking about sex every 5 minutes, if not more. I know I think about it dozens of times a day, but that's because I write about sex for a living. (Or maybe I write about sex for a living because I think about it dozens of times a day.) Either way, my mind spends more time in the gutter than the average woman's. What about you guys?

Coco: I just started dating a guy and we're in that new-relationship sex nirvana stage. All we do is have sex, so I think about it all the time. I get these X-rated flashbacks all day long, and suddenly I'll be sitting there in a trance.

Melissa: How can you function at the restaurant?

Coco: I don't know. It's like I'm on autopilot. I just want to get my shift over with so I can see him again.

Danny: I don't think about sex that much. What I do all day is so unsexy. Maybe 5 or 6 days a month I'll feel horny. But that's it.

Melissa: I think about sex a lot. It's because of the books and magazines I read and the movies I see. I always opt for the steamiest stuff because it keeps my libido rocking.

Danny: Maybe I should start reading Anne Rice instead of Ayn Rand.

Melissa: I'm telling you, it works.

Me: What about seeing a hot guy on the street? Does that trigger lecherous thoughts?

Coco: No, not really. I'll think a guy is hot or good-looking, but I won't imagine getting it on with him. It's too impersonal.

Danny: Me neither.

Melissa: Seeing a hot guy can turn me on, but I won't fantasize about sex with him right then and there. Although, if a guy is at the beach with his shirt off, I might imagine what he'd look like naked.

Me: Women also prepare for sex in ways guys don't. We shave our legs and bikini lines, we moisturize, we put on perfume and sexy lingerie. It's not like we're thinking of our taxes when we do those things. We know what it's all about.

Danny: That's true. When I'm shopping for bras, I think about what would turn a guy on.

Coco: I do that with shoes, too. I'll pick a pair I think he'll find sexy. So basically I'm buying shoes, but thinking about sex.

Melissa: That's so funny. The other day I tried on a necklace that hung down really low and I bought it because I knew this guy I'm seeing would go crazy watching it dangle in my cleavage.

Danny: You know one of the few times I'll think about sex outside of the bedroom? During yoga class.

Coco: Yes! Me too. All those positions that make you bend over and spread your legs? They're so erotic! I can't believe anyone keeps a straight face.

Melissa: Or what about that workout machine for your hamstrings where you lie down on your stomach with your butt in the air?

Danny: Or the inner-thigh machine that you have to open and close your legs to operate?

Coco: And that big exercise ball that you straddle and bounce up and down on? I mean, c'mon. That's a sex toy.

Me: Wow. Guys have no idea how much girls get off at the gym. What about wearing sexy clothes? Do they make you think about sex? Like tall leather boots or fishnet stockings or a miniskirt? Or all three if you don't mind looking like a hooker?

Melissa: I love to wear high-heeled boots because they make me feel like a sex vixen. Sometimes I'll look down at my own legs and think they look pretty damn sexy.

Coco: Yup. Stockings and tights make your legs feel really smooth so that every time you cross and uncross them, it gives you a little thrill.

Melissa: What about driving a stick shift? That kind of turns me on.

Danny: You feel really powerful. Of course, you're also manhandling a large phallic object.

Me: I can't eat a banana or hot dog or lick an ice cream cone without acknowledging the innuendo.

Melissa: I feel sheepish when I'm picking out cucumbers.

Danny: Pervert!

Melissa: You're just in denial.

Coco: One more thing—ever accidentally brush your hand across your own nipple and get turned on by it?

Me: Yup.

Melissa: Yup. Especially when it's cold out and they're already standing at attention.

Coco: Ooh, that's extra nice.

5

BETWEEN
THE SHEETS

Sex from Her Point of View ■
Driving Her Wild ■ Getting What You Want
■ Bells and Whistles

I may write a lot of sex-related articles for such magazines as *Cosmopolitan* and *Men's Health*, but that doesn't make me a sex encyclopedia. So all those technical questions you guys send in (Do penis enlargement pumps really work? What does Viagra do to a clitoris?) are beyond me. What I *can* tell you is just about anything else you want to know about sex from a (relatively) normal woman's perspective—like whether the size of your penis really matters or what your *tongue* can do to a clitoris. And since it can be awkward to talk openly about the deed with the gal you're dating ("So, um, where exactly do you stand on the issue of bondage?"), I pretty much jammed this chapter with priceless information.

Above all, the one thing you need to know about women and sex is that the ability to tell whether we're in the mood for sex on any given night isn't anywhere near as crucial as the ability to tell what *kind* of sex we're in the mood for. If you can pick up on whether she's feeling wild and naughty or sweet and romantic, getting her into bed and blowing her mind will be surprisingly easy. So let me start by clueing you in to what she's thinking . . . and we'll go from there.

■ Sex from Her Point of View

How many men have most women you know been with?

About 10, give or take 5 or 6.

I have a hard time making the first move with a woman—even if she's my girlfriend—because I find it really awkward and never know what will turn her on. How do women want men to initiate sex?

That depends on what kind of mood she's in to start with. If a woman wants to be seduced slowly and gently, she'll send slow-and-gentle signals. She'll hold your hand above the table instead of rubbing your thigh under it, smile sweetly and gaze into your eyes instead of grinning and licking her lips, and talk about how happy she is with your relationship instead of how scrumptious you look in your jeans. She's eager to have sex—only she wants it to feel like "making love." So keep the romantic seduction in first and second gear—stroke her hair, kiss her gently on her collarbone and shoulders, whisper that she's beautiful and smells amazing, lightly caress her body outside her clothes. Things might speed up once both of you get hot and heavy.

Average number of lifetime sex partners . . .
A woman has: **4**
A man has: **12**

(SOURCE: *Men's Health* magazine, May 2002)

Now, if a woman is wearing something incredibly hot (a tight little dress, extra-low-cut shirt, micro mini-skirt, high heels with ankle straps, a push-up bra), if she's flirting overtly with you, touching you a lot, talking in a low, throaty voice, and smiling as if she has a naughty secret, it's because she's feeling damn sexy already. In that mode, a woman doesn't want to be romanced; she wants to be wanted—and wanted bad. So go at her like gangbusters. Be a little aggressive (never forceful)—put your tongue in her mouth and ear, kiss her neck while grabbing her butt and thighs, let her feel your hard-on against her leg. She won't be wearing that micro mini for long.

Why don't women initiate sex more often?

One of the biggest thrills for a girl is knowing that the guy she's hot for finds her irresistibly foxy. So we wait for you to hit on us because it actually makes us hornier than if we hit on you. It also boosts our confidence—since our body turned you on so much that you couldn't hold back, we're more relaxed about flaunting it and bouncing it around for your viewing pleasure. Lastly, we don't initiate as often because we've never really had to. Since we were teenagers, guys have been groping at our waistbands and bras as if convinced the Holy Grail was hidden in one or the other.

Percentage of women who say they initiate sex less than half the time: **33**

Percentage who make the first move about as often as their man: **46**

Percentage who hit on their guy more often than he hits on them: **21**

(SOURCE: cosmomag.com)

If you wish your girl would jump you more often, tell her how much it turns you on when she makes the first move. Tell her it drives you crazy. Tell her she's the sexiest damned thing in the world when she just walks up to you, kisses you hard, and starts pawing at your zipper.

Could you describe what the female orgasm feels like?

Remember the battle scene at the end of *Star Wars* when Luke sends a shot directly into a 2-meter opening in the Death Star to make the whole thing blow? Well, imagine that that shot reaching its target is the beginning of a female orgasm. It may start in that one tiny spot—a.k.a. the clitoris—but the intense rush of pleasure explodes through our entire body, hurtling our brain into space and making us feel like the Force is with us for a few brief moments. At that point, we lose control: Our hips jerk involuntarily, our nipples get hard, and our mouths make an involuntary O. The blast can last anywhere from 5 seconds to a few minutes. Then it slowly fades, and we feel tingly and satisfied all over . . . kind of like the very first time we saw *Star Wars*.

What are women thinking during and after sex?

If you connected a set of speakers to a woman's brain during great sex, you'd hear a string of X-rated sentence fragments. What's coming out of our mouths in the way of moans and squeals and mmmmm-yeah-do-that-baby-ooooooh-my-god is pretty much shooting straight out of our frontal lobes. Without a doubt, the best sex leaves us absolutely brain-dead.

Percentage of women ages 18 to 44 who think about sex every day or several times a day: **19**

Percentage who think about it a few times a week or month: **67**

Percentage who have naughty thoughts less than once a month or never: **14**

(SOURCE: *The Penguin Atlas of Human Sexual Behavior*)

If you tuned in during awkward, nervous, uncomfortable sex, you'd hear stuff more like "Does he like this? I can't tell. Should I try something else? I wonder what he's thinking. Is he looking at my stomach? Do I look fat? What is he doing down there? Can he tell that my last moan was totally fake? Is he faking?" Naturally after crummy sex we feel self-conscious and embarrassed—and therefore need to cuddle even more than usual to be reassured that one night of low-grade nookie isn't going to rattle the relationship. If it's a random hookup that turns out to be a flop, we'll want to take off pronto and pretend it never happened.

Are drunken booty calls flattering or completely annoying?

That depends on who it is you call. If you dial someone you've just started sleeping with because you just can't stop thinking about her, she'll probably be flattered—especially if you mention that you ". . . just can't stop thinking about her." Long-term girlfriends are more complicated—does she have to get up early for work the next day, mind if you taste like beer and cigarettes, want sex as much as you do? Still, I'd say girlfriends are pretty flattered to find out they're on your mind at the end of the night.

As for ex-girlfriends who have mixed feelings about you, or women you've had casual sex with a couple of times, it's a total crapshoot. When in doubt, call those types on their cell instead of their home phones. Don't have her cell number? Then you shouldn't be booty-calling her.

A girl I'm sleeping with makes coy references to the fact that she masturbates a lot. Does that mean she isn't getting enough sex, or does she just really like to play solo?

In my experience, women who love to blab about how sexually active they are usually have an agenda. Either she's trying to tantalize you by presenting herself as the kind of sex-hungry siren men fantasize about their whole lives or—and your instincts would be right—she wants more sex with you but doesn't feel comfortable asking for it point-blank. Another hint: If she already initiates sex more than you do, it's probably the latter.

Why do so many women insist on turning out the lights before having sex?

Two of the reasons a woman might want to get it on in the dark:

1. She's self-conscious or insecure about her body, and a pitch-black room allows her to relax and have fun because what you don't see won't turn you off. (Yes, I know, the chances you'd be turned off by a nude female body are slim to zip, but women with body-image problems have a hard time believing that.)

Percentage of women who think sex is better with the lights off: **35**
Percentage who would rather get an eyeful: **65**

(SOURCE: cosmomag.com)

2. She finds doing it in the dark more mysterious and romantic—it's just easier to drown in sensual pleasure when you can't see the water stains on the ceiling.

How can I convince a woman to have sex with the lights on?

Start by having sex with one candle by the bed, then two, then three. Candlelight is surprisingly bright and endlessly flattering.

Tell her over and over again how beautiful every inch of her body looks and how exciting it is to see her while you make love to her. Not only will she slowly stop thinking of light as her enemy; she'll start thinking of it as an aphrodisiac for you—and for her.

Why do you think women don't want to have sex as often as men do? How can I find a woman who's as horny as I am?

On the contrary, I think women do get randy as much as men do—but only when they're with a guy who's fantastic in bed. If a woman knew that every time she had sex with her boyfriend her clitoris was going to end up on cloud nine, he'd be getting jumped more often than a trampoline in the backyard of a house filled with hyperactive pre-teens. So your strategy shouldn't be to find a sex-crazed female; it should be to create one by being so damn good she can't get enough of you.

> Percentage of women who like to have sex two times a week or less: **18**
> Percentage who want it three to five times a week: **48**
> Percentage who prefer to do it six or more times a week: **35**
>
> (SOURCE: COSMOMAG.COM)

Are women turned off by uncircumcised penises?

Something like 80 percent of American guys were snipped as babes, so foreskins aren't something most American women think about at all—until we discover one in a guy's pants. One friend whose ex-boyfriend had a hooded johnson confessed that, because he was always hard when, um, push came to shove, she didn't even notice until she'd been sleeping with him for 2 months. When she finally played with it at rest, she said it was "interesting and kind of exotic." Another friend, who has never laid eyes on a lance with a lid, said she'd be fascinated—and intimidated because she wouldn't know how to handle it. Her exact words? "He'd have to show me what it does!"

I think the honest answer to your question is that most women are very curious and a little clueless—but not at all turned off.

We know condom-free sex is way more enjoyable for you guys—because skin on skin is leaps and bounds better for us, too. But if you don't automatically reach for one in the heat of the moment, we'll assume you never use protection unless you have to—which means you're probably a walking disease. You'll also reveal yourself as someone who has a hard time doing the right thing under pressure ("Hello, future liar/cheater!"). So don't wait till she asks you to wear a jacket over your jimmy. Just wear one.

If I have sex with a woman during her period, will it hurt her? Can she get pregnant? Will the blood get everywhere?

Don't worry, it won't hurt her. As a matter of fact, the analgesic effect of an orgasm can help alleviate her cramps and boost her mood. (A college friend of mine swears that sex is the only cure for her raging PMS.) The week a woman has her period is also the week she's least likely to get pregnant. It's still possible, but because her uterus is in reset mode (think of it as an oven that automatically self-cleans every month), it's highly unlikely. And unless you're having sex on the first or second day of her period, there probably won't be much blood at all. Putting a towel down on the bed is a good idea if you're worried about staining the sheets. She won't be offended.

■ Driving Her Wild

Tell me the truth: Do bigger penises really feel that much better?

Dirk Diggler members are like Dolly Parton knockers—sure, they sell magazines, but in reality they're more than any one person wants or knows what to do with. Even my most over-sexed female friends agree that size matters only if the organ in question is way too big (think a standard-issue flashlight) or way too small (think a standard-issue stogie) to be of any use. Vaginas, in case you didn't know, will expand or contract to fit what's inside them, which explains why a tiny tampon will stay put even after pregnancy. Aesthetically speaking, like breasts, penises of all shapes and sizes can provide the same amount of pleasure (yes, even the ones that hang a serious left or right)—especially when attached to a man who has a lot more going for him than a killer unit.

Length of the average erect penis: **6.4 inches**
Circumference of the average erect penis: **5 inches**

(SOURCE: The Definitive Size Survey, sizesurvey.com)

What kind of attention do women want paid to their breasts?

Lots and all kinds—except the kind you'd give to one of those rubber stress balls or a guacamole-bound avocado. The robotic squeeze-release, squeeze-release move doesn't do a thing for us.

What does work? Definitely flick our nipples with your tongue and tease them with your fingertips until they get hard. Hold them in both hands and massage them, using slow, circular motions while kissing them. Lightly caress the outer curves—most guys forget to pay attention to the sides of the breasts. If she's sitting or standing, actually lifting them so you support their weight can feel great, too. During sex, if you gently pinch a nipple (or both), it feels fantastic, as does caressing our breasts anytime during the deed. When not in bed or heading there, we love to have our breasts lovingly touched at surprising times, like when we're making break-fast or reading the paper. I once had a boyfriend who would suddenly pull down the neckline of my shirt and kiss both nipples in a flash. It made me laugh and turned me on in an instant.

Does a woman enjoy sex even if she doesn't orgasm?

An orgasm is only the last 15 seconds of what is usually an all-around amazing experience. Okay, it's the best 15 seconds. But if it's just not happening, most women are happy to call it quits and shift down—as long as that's not a frequent occurrence.

Whatever you do, don't give up before she does, or she'll think you don't care about satisfying her. What do you do when you're about to pass Go and collect $200 but she's stuck in Free Parking? Ask if she wants to climb on top—most women climax easier that way. If she declines, she probably doesn't mind sitting this one out. Or you could let your orgasm rip and then focus the energy you have left on stimulating her manually. If she pushes her body urgently against your hand or starts kissing you passionately, she's still game and is getting close. If she's had enough, she'll gently move your hand away.

As much as women ooh and ah over Sting's alleged ability to have sex for 70 hours straight, we'd rather save our energy than exhaust ourselves—and you— over one elusive orgasm.

What does the female orgasm feel like?

I get this question a lot. Which is why I'm answering it twice. If my *Star Wars* analogy on page 87 wasn't enough for you, here's a food-related one.

Imagine someone is dripping warm pudding onto the most

Percentage of women who report reaching orgasm during sex with their primary partner . . .
Always: **29**
Usually: **42**
Sometimes: **21**
Rarely or never: **5**

Percentage of women who reach orgasm most often through . . .
Manual stimulation: **50**
Oral sex: **47**
When she's on top: **36**
When he's on top: **34**

Percentage of women who are "very satisfied" with their sex lives who reached orgasm at least once every sexual encounter: **46**

Percentage of women who think simultaneous orgasm is necessary for gratifying sex: **14**

(SOURCES: *The Penguin Atlas of Human Sexual Behavior*, *What Women Want*, *Men's Health* magazine, May 2002)

OUR SEX SECRETS | What We Would Tell You If Only We Had the Guts

I really want to try kinky things. I just don't want him to think I'm a slut or assume that just because I want him to tie me up, I also want to have a threesome someday. I feel like guys think you're either a goody-two-shoes or a total freak, and they need to understand that most women are somewhere in between."

—*Danielle, 28 (attached)*

"I'm most impressed by guys who want to do it two or more times in the same night."

—*Trisha, 21 (single)*

"He takes the 'sensitive male' thing too far. I just want him to attack me once in a while."

—*Jamie-Lynn, 26 (attached)*

"I'd love it if he would trim his pubic hair. It's really long and bushy and gets in the way when I'm trying to go down on him."

—*Caryn, 25 (attached)*

sensitive spot on your body, a.k.a. your penis. Now imagine that erotic sensation spreading from there to your thighs, abdomen, and chest. You can hardly take how good it feels to have your body engulfed by this warmth. Now, just when you're sure it can't get any better, you sense something wonderful coming, and it's getting closer and closer and the anticipation is killing you, then— *wo-o-o-o-osh!*—a steaming pudding tsunami washes over you, your brain goes blank, muscles deep inside you start throbbing ecstatically, and every nerve from your toes to your tongue reverberates with gooey, delicious pleasure. That's kind of what it feels like. (Does that make you want some pudding now, or what?)

"I like my nipples nibbled on."

—*Camilla, 32 (single)*

"Men never pay enough attention to my butt. I want it squeezed, caressed, spanked, kissed, licked, bit, and anything else he can think of."

—*Patricia, 28 (single)*

"When the girl is on top, guys should massage our breasts, stroke our pubic hair, and otherwise keep their hands on our bodies, instead of just lying there."

—*Tina, 23 (single)*

"I wish my boyfriend would ask me to do daring things more often, like have sex on the roof, in the car, in the bathroom at a bar. I'm dying to do that stuff, but I'm afraid he won't be into it."

—*Cheryl, 22 (attached)*

"Rub my clitoris! Rub it hard!"

—*Gretchen, 26 (single)*

What sex positions do women like best?

Women who are confident about their curves and aren't too shy to call the shots in bed favor the woman-on-top position. For most of us, it's the surest way to orgasm because it provides the most control and clitoral stimulation (which we get by grinding against your abdomen like we're trying to start a campfire). Demure or less experienced women prefer to let the man lead, which makes missionary position perfect. And if they're at all self-conscious about their body, missionary keeps the tummy looking flat, and the butt and thighs out of the picture.

Do women prefer slow sex?

I'm glad you asked because I've had more than one friend complain to me that their too sensitive boyfriend never grabs them,
bends them over a sturdy chair, and gives it to them like they
mean it. You see, even in a loving, trusting relationship, a little
aggression can be a major turn-on. Yeah, we want slow and
gentle sometimes. But a lot of other nights, fast and hard feels
even better.

What does a woman want when it comes to oral sex?

Variety and vigor.

Lick her like you're devouring an ice cream cone. Spell out the
alphabet on her clitoris with your tongue. Hum the Canadian
national anthem. Lick the area immediately around the clitoris
and especially just above where the clitoral hood starts, using a
decent amount of pressure. Pay attention to clit location at all
times. Expose it, using your thumb to pull up the clitoral hood
and keep it out of the way. Or slide a finger or two inside her as
you lick her clitoris (she'll go crazy for that, I swear). Throw her
a curve: Lick up and down, side to side, make tiny figure eights,
wax on/wax off. Apply pressure to the front (pubic hair side)
wall of her vagina, making little circles or pressing and releasing
as if on a button. You'll have to read her movements, moans, and
sighs (or simply ask outright) to know if she wants you to
change speed or pressure. But putting this advice into practice
will get you off to one hell of a great start.

I can give her an orgasm orally every time, but never via pene-tration. Do you think she's unfulfilled?

The fact that you can give her an orgasm at all is fabulous. Period. Would she prefer to come with you inside of her? Probably.
That doesn't mean she's unsatisfied. Instead of worrying, why
not let her know that you're willing to try anything to make her
peak in other ways? If oral sex usually does the trick, your girl
obviously needs a lot of direct clitoral contact to make that
happen. Here's a tip: While she's on her stomach, enter her from

behind, keeping most of your weight on your elbows or hands (so that she can move her hips freely) and suggest that she use her own hands to stimulate her clitoris as much as she likes. The intense clitoral contact combined with the feeling of you moving back and forth may be enough to send her over the edge.

■ Getting What You Want

What are some ways to initiate sex when you can tell it's the furthest thing from her mind?

Draw her a bubble bath. Give her a massage. Wrestle.

She says it's a turnoff when I ask for oral sex. But if I don't ask, I don't get. Any tips?

There really is no right way to ask, except for maybe a gently whispered . . . no, even that sounds like porn cheese.

Okay, this probably isn't the answer you're looking for, but the best way to get oral sex is to give it—and the more enthusiastic you are, the more likely she'll want to know what all the fun's about. Go down on her for a lo-o-o-ong time one night; then see if she returns the favor the next time. Or, while you're down there, swing your body so that you're lying sideways next to her, your penis only four or five tongue lengths away. Hopefully, she'll go for the bait. *Do not* slide into a version of 69 with you on top since giving her a mouthful of pubes and a proctologist's-eye view of your butt isn't going to help your cause any.

Subtler tactics? Gently slip your finger in her mouth during a long, wet kiss, or suck on her fingers and toes to get her mind on the right track. If none of that works, it's time for desperate measures: Stop going down on her entirely. If she asks for it, use her request as an opportunity to find out once and for all why she won't go south. But brace yourself: Her answer may be that she's not into it and never will be because she simply doesn't enjoy it. Maybe she had a horrible experience in the past that she just can't get over, or maybe having something that big in her mouth activates her gag reflex. If either is the case, you'll have to decide whether or not she's worth the sacrifice.

If a woman is going down on a guy and he wants her to use her hands or go slower or faster, what's the best way to make that request?

She won't mind if you whisper simple requests in the heat of the moment. Just be sure to use a soft, low, sexy voice and tell her how fantastic it feels immediately after she does it.

As for more complicated moves, it's better to wait until you're lying in bed together postpassion, talking openly about sex. (If you don't talk openly about sex, that's going to have to change.) As with any sex conversation, be sure to let her know right off the bat how wonderful she is in bed and how outrageously good she makes you feel. Once her ego is nice and inflated, mention how great you imagine it would feel if she did X and Y while doing Z. Describe the move in general and then as she asks you questions, get more specific. Never, ever imply (or admit) that you've done that very thing with someone else. And don't let on that you planned this conversation—the idea just occurred to you, right? As you have more and more talks like this one, they'll get easier and easier —until eventually you can ask each other to try just about anything.

> Percentage of women who are willing to perform fellatio: **50 to 80**
>
> Percentage who find it pleasurable: **35 to 65**
>
> (SOURCE: *The Kinsey Institute New Report on Sex*)

Why is it that some women swallow and some spit? Is there anything I can do to make a woman feel more comfortable about getting it down the hatch?

Women who swallow do so because they truly like it, or because they know what a huge turn-on it is for guys and enjoy providing that extra bit of pleasure.

But you shouldn't be surprised that some women are squeamish. It could be the taste, the consistency, or the idea that there are more than a million little sperm swimming around in a single teaspoon that turns them off. Or a woman might just find it bizarre and/or humiliating to eat body fluids. Ask your resident spitter why she doesn't like it. It could be that she doesn't even realize how much it matters to you. (Why does it matter to you, anyway? Is it really that important? Would you be willing to do it if the roles were reversed?) If taste is the problem, I've heard that you can make your sperm more palatable by eating more fruits and vegetables and less red meat. But listen, given that she's going down on you in the first place, is it really worth making a big deal out of whether or not she digests your DNA?

The average ejaculation chemically consists of protein, citric acid, fructose, sodium, chloride, ammonia, ascorbic acid, acid phosphatase, calcium, carbon dioxide, cholesterol, prostaglandins, creatine, other minerals, and numerous other chemicals—but has a total of only 5 calories.

(SOURCE: *The Kinsey Institute New Report on Sex*)

Is there any way to find out if a woman would be willing to have anal sex without coming right out and asking her?

Let me first warn you that most women I know are absolutely opposed to rear-exit entry and would be horrified if anyone but a very long-term boyfriend tried it. If your gal hasn't shown enthusiasm about experimentation, don't test her boundaries with this trick. Try 69 instead, or some unusual sex position (ever hear of the wheelbarrow?).

If you're with a girl who's always game for something new, the least pervy way to find out if she likes anal stimulation is to slide a slick finger back there when you're in the vicinity and lightly circle her anus with it, then ask her if that feels okay. If she says yes with enthusiasm and pushes her body toward you, then you should slip your finger in (just a little!) and gauge her reaction. If it's positive, then there's a good chance she's not grossed out or turned off by anal sex. Go very slow to give her time to figure out what you're up to and plenty of chances to say stop. If she quickly pulls away and gets quiet or upset when you approach her back door with your finger, then obviously she isn't into this sort of adventure.

How can I encourage a woman to take control and be more dominant?

After you start kissing her and caressing her as usual, whisper in her ear that you want her to tell you what makes her feel good. She might giggle or not know what you mean at first, but tell her you're serious—you really want her to order you around. If she still hesitates, ask her a question like "Does it feel good when I do this?" and then lick her breasts, say, or nip her earlobe. When she says yes, ask her what else will make her feel good. Keep your tone playful but sexy.

Another option is at the end of a stressful day (for you, not her), throw yourself back on the couch and tell her: 1) how much you want her, 2) how tired you are, 3) how much you wish she would take off her clothes and have her way with you. Then kiss her passionately, but otherwise don't lift a finger.

What can I do or say to show her that she can just relax and get freaky if she wants to?

Normally conservative women get wild in bed with two types of men: the ones they don't care about and the ones they're completely in love with. We'll let loose with the former because we don't care what the guy thinks of us. With the latter, it's because we feel 100 percent safe and comfortable.

Percentage of women who are turned on by erotic talk: **79**

(SOURCE: canoe.ca)

With a long-term girlfriend who's always been conservative in bed, start tame and build up to freaky. Wait until some Friday or Saturday night when she's got a little wine buzz going and whisper in her ear that you want to have sex with her on the kitchen table. If she blushes but smiles, make that whisper a reality ASAP. Raise the bar slowly but steadily, always on a night when she's laughing a lot, feeling loose and relaxed, and obviously in love.

If you want to get a one-night stand or an occasional hookup to go nuts, lead by example. Moan loudly, tell her what to do in a sultry voice, change from doggy style to missionary to cowgirl in less than 10 minutes, spank her butt gently—and let her know she can reciprocate any way she likes.

■ Bells and Whistles

How do women feel about using lubricant during sex? What's the best way to get a woman to use it if she doesn't already?

Lube is fantastic. I think it's the best sex enhancer on the planet—but it's true that until a woman tries it, she might be a bit put off. You see, a woman's first lubricant experience usually is at the gynecologist's office when the doc squirts a dollop of K-Y Jelly onto a gloved hand before the examination—not a real sexy association. (She also might be concerned that you don't think she's getting wet enough on her own, making her feel somehow inadequate.)

There is something about the K-Y brand that seems very clean and good and safe, unlike say "Jimmy's Love Juice" or some other adult entertainment–sounding brand. So when you break out the slick stuff for the first time, I'd highly recommend K-Y Liquid Silk—same brand, sexier image—as a female-friendly lube. Let her see the bottle outside the bedroom rather than springing it on her midcoitus. Maybe leave it on the kitchen table, where it's bound to catch her eye and inspire a question. Which is when you get to explain that you want to find out if it makes her feel as good as the ads say it will.

Should I be insulted if the girl I'm seeing uses a vibrator?

No. A vibrator is a harmless little orgasm machine, and using it is about as close to having sex with someone you're attracted to as watching *Apollo 13* is to experiencing space flight.

It's ironic that vibrators are sometimes called "personal massagers" in catalogs that don't want to use the word "vibrator" because a vibrator really is a personal massager and nothing

MISSION: MULTIPLE ORGASMS
Six Steps for Reaching Her Peak Potential

You can make her come three or four times in one night, but it's going to take some work. Here's how to do it.

1. Discover her hot spots. The more of her pleasure points you stimulate, the more excited she's going to get, so pay attention to the places on her body that respond to sexual touch. Kiss her neck, suck her toes, play with her nipples, massage her butt—see which get the biggest rise out of her.

2. Dive tongue first. Many women report coming during oral sex more frequently than any other kind.

3. Stop and start. This is the most crucial tactic to helping your partner achieve multiple orgasms. Arouse her to the point of low to moderate excitement and then back off until she calms down, but not completely. Then increase stimulation until she's slightly more aroused than she was the first time, but backing off well before she nears orgasm. Continue slowly increasing the level of her arousal and backing off before she comes. When she finally does peak, her sexual energy will be through the roof. Immediately following her orgasm, begin stimulating her again to stop her

more—it just so happens that this particular type of massage ends in an orgasm. It's an efficient masturbation tool because it requires zero energy to hold the thing against our clitoris and visualize some sexy scenario. It usually doesn't take long before the intense buzzing sensation sends a wave of pleasurable spasms throughout our lower body. As a matter of fact, if you're with a woman who takes forever to orgasm, a vibrator could be your new best friend. Using it in addition to your usual licks and tricks could cut your labor in half.

arousal from subsiding. Start the turn-on/back-off game again until she builds up to another orgasm.

4. Hit her G-spot. Many multiorgasmic women say that their first orgasms revolve around their clitoris, while later ones feel more vaginal. After she's had her first orgasm, enter her from behind (with her on her hands and knees or lying on her stomach) and thrust slowly and rhythmically. The head of your penis will be massaging the front wall of her vagina, where the G-spot is located.

5. Man her clit. Stimulating her clitoris during intercourse will only up the chances that she'll orgasm numerous times. If your hand gets tired, encourage her to touch herself, or use a vibrator to give her a continuous buzz.

6. Keep communications open. If she knows what would make her come at any given moment, so can you. Continue to ask her what feels best, and eventually she'll be comfortable enough to just tell you what she wants and when she wants it.

(SOURCE: *The Multi-Orgasmic Couple* by Mantak Chia, Maneewan Chia, Douglas Abrams, and Rachel Carlton Abrams, M.D.)

What's the deal with multiple orgasms? Do all women experience these?

Not even close. The ability to come two or more times in a row is as rare as being able to hit a fastball in the majors. The reason most women can't is that the clitoris becomes extremely sensitive after orgasm, making any further stimulation almost painful. Many other women don't even try to come a second time because they'd rather relax and enjoy the afterglow. As for those rare women who can round home base over and over again, shall we start a wave?

I've never met a woman who likes to engage in role-play. Why is that?

Prancing around in a French maid's outfit might be fine for Halloween, but it does seem a little over the top for a random Tuesday night. Sure, sex should be fun and playful and even downright silly sometimes, but a little Cheez Whiz, a few freckles, and a game of connect the dots can make that happen. Dressing up in costumes and playing pretend almost seems like too much effort just for a quick thrill. I talked about this with a few friends and we agreed that we'd simply feel too ridiculous to get turned on. (Ask us again after we've been with the same guy for 10 years, though, and we'll have probably changed our minds.)

What would make a girl feel comfortable having sex in the great outdoors? I've always wanted to get it on at the beach, in the woods, in my backyard.

Any woman who loves getting it on in every room in the house and also enjoys stuff like hiking and camping will be psyched to have sex outside, as long as there's some privacy and something comfortable and clean to rest her body on (so bring a blanket).

If she's less adventurous than average and won't sit on a rock without asking you to cover it with your jacket first, you face more of a challenge. You may have to introduce her to wilderness whoopee by taking her to a luxury cabin in the woods—the kind of place with a secluded deck and hot tub, and equipped with fancy extras like robes, slippers, and wineglasses. It's weird logic, but if a place is swank enough, outdoor sex will seem extravagant and romantic instead of risky or dirty.

Some of my buddies say they trim or shave the hair on their privates. I've never had any complaints before, but they tell me it's "common courtesy" and women like it. Is this something you or your girlfriends see a lot? Do women like when a guy shaves?

If your patch is so long and thick it could be harvested to make Gene Shalit toupees, by all means trim it. (Perk: Short pubic hair makes your penis look longer.) But unless you're already involved with a woman you know will find it sexy, don't shave it all off. Unlike the thrill you might get when a date turns out hairless, a shaved guy comes off as a wannabe John Holmes, which is more pathetic than provocative to the average girl.

NO BOYZ ALLOWED Go Off-Limits Online

Sneak a peek at these women-only Web sites. It's a great way to find out even more about what makes our bodies melt, what our wildest fantasies are, which sex toys we like, what we worry about in bed, et cetera. You might even get turned on in the process.

Goodvibes.com This San Francisco–based online sex boutique is owned and run by women for women. Chicks who never would be caught dead walking into an adult bookstore come here to purchase erotic books and movies as well as vibrators and other sex toys of all shapes and sizes.

Cakenyc.com A hot Web site for 20-something women who party hard and love to express their sexuality. Cake's mission is to create an atmosphere where women feel comfortable confessing their every desire and openly debating some of the most controversial sex topics on the table today. Their fantasy page reveals just how horny women can get.

Cosmomag.com The primary source of information about sex for most women of the civilized world, Cosmo is a gold mine for discovering the naughty/catty/silly stuff that women talk about with their best friends. Plus it frequently publishes Kama Sutra–style guides to sex positions.

Definitely consider sliding a razor carefully over your scrotum and whatever stray hairs sprout out of your penis. Women will appreciate how much smoother you feel to their hands and tongue. Some tips: Lay a warm, wet washcloth over the area you want to shave (or take a warm bath) to soften the coarse hairs, and always use shaving cream or soap. Oh, and one other thing: When you shave a part of your body for the first time, it usually feels itchy as hell when the hair starts to grow back. It'll fade after a few weeks, but until then expect to paw at your package more than usual.

How can I get my girlfriend to try a little light bondage?

If you're not comfortable simply asking her how she feels about being playfully tied up, try "accidentally" leaving two neckties on a bedside table. While you're fooling around, tell her you want her to lie still while you kiss her all over. Then have her stretch her arms over her head while you give her all sorts of wonderful attention with your lips and tongue. After you've made her wriggle and moan, tell her it's her turn to do the same to you—but since you don't trust yourself to stay still and keep your hands to yourself, she's going to have to tie your wrists to the bed. Letting her tie you up first will show her it's just for fun, and she'll see that the neckties are thick and soft enough to be comfy and easy to slip out of.

GIRLS OVERHEARD:
The Female Orgasm

The Scene

Sandra's huge loft apartment with an amazing view of Wall Street on a Friday night. We're meeting here for cocktails before going to a party. Some of us are more comfortable talking about this than others. But the cocktails definitely make it easier!

The Guest List

Sandra, 26, an interior designer
Caitlin, 23, just got a job as an assistant television producer
Christine, 31, owns a French restaurant
Felicia, 29, a makeup artist and amateur salsa dancer

Me: Has anyone ever faked an orgasm?

Felicia: Of course! How else can you end bad sex quickly?

Christine: Ouch!

Sandra: I've done it because I actually felt bad that I couldn't come. It's awful when a guy is trying everything he can think of and it's still not happening. If I don't fake it, he'll feel inadequate for not getting the job done and I'll feel inadequate, too.

Me: But then you still don't have an orgasm and now the guy thinks what he was doing actually works!

Sandra: I know. It just makes things worse. But at that moment you just want it to be over. Especially if you're not in a relationship with the guy. Why bother getting into a big conversation about it? I don't think I'd fake it with a guy I was seriously involved with.

Christine: I'll fake an orgasm every once in a while when I don't think I'm going to be able to have one but don't want to explain why. It's also because I want a guy to think I'm great in bed. I figure a lot of men equate being orgasmic with being sexual.

Felicia: Honey, I know exactly what you're saying. Men love watching a woman in the throes of pleasure. And I think they consider a woman who comes sexier than one who doesn't.

Caitlin: I've never faked an orgasm. I'll just tell my boyfriend it isn't going to happen tonight. He knows he's still making me feel really good; it's just that I'm not relaxed enough or for some physical reason my body can't manage it.

Sandra: It's great that you're honest about it.

Me: Yeah. Because I think men really want to know how to make a woman come, and faking it just sends them mixed signals.

But I do understand about wanting him to think you're orgasmic/sexy.

Caitlin: Orgasms are just really hard for me. I need clitoral and vaginal stimulation to make it happen, which means one of us has to keep a hand rubbing my clitoris at all times during sex.

Felicia: What about when you're on top?

Caitlin: That's easier, for sure.

Me: What do you think guys do wrong when they try to give us orgasms?

Felicia: For one thing, they don't use enough variety. Think of all the ways they like their penises to be handled and licked. I'm not all that different! I want a lot of different strokes and amounts of pressure from a guy's fingers and tongue.

Sandra: And then at the end, they usually want you to maintain a steady pace and pressure so they can come. That's exactly what I need, too.

Caitlin: I have to be completely relaxed to have an orgasm, so I need long, slow sex. And I don't expect to get off during a quickie.

Me: What's the best way for a guy to learn what works for you?

Felicia: He needs to watch you touch yourself and ask a lot of questions about what you like.

Sandra: If he puts his hand over yours while you're touching yourself to get an idea of the way you do it, he'd learn a lot.

Caitlin: My problem is that I don't know exactly what makes me come. I feel like it's something different every time.

Felicia: But there's always friction, honey.

Sandra: And you have to be wet. He should lick his fingers if he has to, or use lube.

Me: What about orgasms during intercourse alone?

Sandra: Certain positions work better for me, like when I'm on top or during missionary when I bend my legs up to my chest. Or if I straddle him in a sitting position. Because basically they're positions where my clit rubs against his body.

Felicia: Another good position is when the guy lies on top of you but you keep your legs squeezed together. It's not easy for him to get his penis in, but once it is, it will rub your clitoris every time it slides in and out.

Me: What about the G-spot? Fact or fiction?

Felicia: I think there's some truth to the G-spot. But it's not a spot, right? Isn't it more of an area on the front wall of the vagina?

Caitlin: Yeah. I've heard that some women can come from G-spot stimulation alone.

Felicia: Yup. I can. Either when a man uses his fingers or if his penis hits that area directly.

Me: If you lie on your stomach with your legs together and he lies on top of you and enters you from behind—kind of the reverse of that position Felicia was describing—that's supposed to be a great G-spot position. Missionary is great, too, if the guy is kneeling.

Sandra: The important thing that guys need to know is that it takes experimentation to figure out what makes any one woman orgasm. No single formula works every time.

Caitlin: And when in doubt, they should ask.

Felicia: Yes, ask. We're dying to tell them what to do.

6

BREAKUPS AND BLOW-OFFS

Blow-Offs: The How-To ▪
Ending a Long-Term Relationship
▪ When You're Dumped

S o it's breakup time. Maybe you flipped to this chapter because you're about to leave someone in the dust and you want to know how to let her down easy. If that's the case, good—because it's a small, small world and the woman you dump today could turn out to be tight with your boss, your accountant, your surgeon, or, worse, the woman you're dying to date next. Someday you might even realize she's the closest you ever came to finding your dream girl and want her to take you back (don't shake your head—you never know!). Most important, the more kindness you bestow during the breakup, the less likely you'll be to find your favorite pet boiling on your kitchen stove courtesy of a psycho ex with a sick revenge streak.

You also could be checking out this section because you got dumped yourself and want to find out why, figure out how to win her back, or get over her as fast as possible. No matter what your situation, the advice I'm about to dish out can help you avoid the unnecessary pain usually associated with rejection (both giving and receiving)—and get straight to the part where you bounce back even happier than you were before.

Blow-Offs: The How-To

How can I tell a woman I'm not attracted to her without hurting her feelings?

The news that you're not hot for her is bound to make all but the most secure woman's self-esteem sink faster than Kevin Costner's reputation after *Waterworld*. Her feelings will be hurt no matter how you get the message across. So throw her ego a lifeline: Soften the bad news with compliments. Tell her you realize a lot of men would kill for a chance to date a sweet/sexy/intelligent/funny woman like her, but right now you're just not looking for anything more than friendship (leave the "with her" part out). Or claim that for whatever inexplicable reason—and in spite of the fact that you think she's amazing—the chemistry just isn't there. That old "It's not you . . ." line may be cliché, but when you're on the receiving end of rejection, it's what you need to hear.

Sometimes I don't return a woman's calls after a few dates as a way of letting her know I'm not interested. Just recently a woman called me a "pathetic jerk" for not being more up-front. Is there a more humane, but equally painless, way to get the message across?

The trick to doling out rejection without damaging a woman's confidence or making her resent you is to act as if she's just as underwhelmed by you. Even if you suspect that's not the case, it's a way of helping her save face. So say something like "I'm not sure we should go out again since it didn't seem like sparks were flying—no doubt you feel the same way. But I wanted to let you know how much I enjoyed meeting you. I'd hate to lose touch completely just because the dating thing didn't work out." If she's hurt and disappointed, she probably won't show it (until she puts down the receiver and starts bawling her eyes out). And you definitely will have not been a "pathetic jerk."

I have a girlfriend and am not looking to cheat, but a female friend of mine keeps flirting and dropping hints that she wouldn't mind hooking up with me. How can I make it clear that's not going to happen without ruining our friendship?

Tell this friend how much you care about your girlfriend and how happy you are with her. Come right out and tell her that her "hints" make you uncomfortable. She isn't going to stop being your friend just because you aren't willing to deceive someone you care about.

The bottom line: If she thinks you're the cheating type, she obviously doesn't know you very well. And if she's trying to cause problems between you and your girlfriend, it doesn't sound to me like she's being a very good friend.

I'm going abroad for 6 months and I want to be open to meeting women when I'm there. Think I could get my girlfriend to agree to a relationship hiatus?

She'll never go for it. She may even break up with you just for suggesting it.

Unless . . . you just recently started dating and neither of you is sure you want to commit to the other. In that case, you probably could convince her that since things between you are still up in the air, it wouldn't make sense to be committed while you were away. But a serious girlfriend will take your plea for an infidelity permit as a sign you're not trustworthy and not really into her—and she'll be right on both counts.

Percentage of Americans who admit they've been dumped/rejected at least two to three times during their lifetimes: **46**

Percentage who say they've dumped/rejected 6 to 10 significant others: **22**

(SOURCE: *USA Today*, February 2, 2002)

Listen, just break up with this woman before you head overseas because it sounds to me like you're going to cheat whether you have her blessing or not. If you want to be free, be free. If you want to be involved and act like you're free, wake up—because that kind of stuff happens only in your dreams.

If a girl doesn't return a phone call or e-mail, does it mean she's blowing you off?

Ninety-nine percent of the time, yes. But there's always the slim chance she didn't get your message, so there's no harm (or loss of dignity) in calling or e-mailing one last time to ask her what's up. If you still don't hear back, without a doubt she's out of the picture. Any attempt to contact her again will just be a waste of your time.

I was set up with a girl who'd expressed an interest in dating me. We went out, everything went fine, and she even kissed me good night (a long one, too). She told her friends she had a great time. Then a few days later she told me she's not ready for a relationship. What happened?

I'm thinking the same thing you are: "Not ready for a relationship? Then why did she request the setup in the first place?" While a woman occasionally feels obligated to give a guy a peck at the end of a date, she won't get her tongue involved if she doesn't sincerely enjoy your company. She was definitely into you, so you should be suspicious of some outside factor.

Regardless of her crappy excuse, don't take the rejection personally. As for what changed her mind, the reason could be anything from a resurfaced ex to a family problem that will consume her for the next couple of months. If the person who introduced you can't shed light on this mystery, call her once, and only once. Tell her you had a great time and understand she's having second thoughts—you're just wondering if she's okay. You never know—maybe she'll open up and explain the situation. You might even have an amazing, intimate conversation and decide to meet up again next Saturday for a romantic dinner. If she starts sounding like you do when you're lying to some chick about why you don't want to see her again, cut the conversation short and move on.

What does it mean if a woman says she doesn't want to date you but then offers to fix you up with one of her friends?

Take it as a huge compliment. I've done this before and it was because in spite of the fact that the guy in question was cute, interesting, and fun, he just wasn't my type. Still he was so great that I couldn't bear to let him walk away without introducing him to a few of my single friends whose ideal man is different from mine. Sure, you might feel like you're being pimped, but it's still a great opportunity to meet other women.

CALLOUS VS. COY Is She Blowing You Off or Playing Hard to Get?

Think you can tell the difference? Circle B if you think the action is a blow-off or G if you think she's playing games. Then check your answers below.

1. She waits at least 1 day before returning calls.   B G

2. You ask her out for that night and she says she's busy.   B G

3. She sends you one-word answers to e-mails.   B G

4. She mentions three times how incredibly busy work is these days.   B G

5. She won't go home with you after the third date.   B G

6. She vaguely refers to another guy in her life.   B G

7. You suggest doing something 2 weeks in the future and she says "maybe."   B G

8. She vehemently insists on splitting the dinner bill on the first date.   B G

Answers: 1:G, 2:G, 3:B, 4:B, 5:G, 6:G, 7:B, 8:B

■ Ending a Long-Term Relationship

How can you tell if you should break up with someone or just keep trying to work things out?

Sit down for a second and imagine yourself without her. Day after day goes by and you don't see her or talk to her at all. And it isn't because she's just away for a few weeks on vacation without you—this time she's never, ever coming back. Now, how do you picture yourself? Relieved not to have to deal with relationship problems, having a blast with your friends, meeting great new women, and pretty much happier without her? Or do you imagine yourself relieved not to have to deal with relationship problems, but otherwise missing her like crazy, wishing she were around to talk to, go to dinner/the movies/the park with, have late-night/early-morning sex with, just sit around and do nothing with?

> Bad relationships negatively affect job performance, physical and mental health, financial security, and even life span.
>
> (SOURCE: *Psychology Today*, May/June 2002)

If it's the latter, keep trying to work things out because you still love her and she still makes you happy—most of the time.

I broke up with my girlfriend more than 2 months ago and she's still a total wreck. How can I get her to stop calling and expecting me to make her feel better?

Do her a big favor and refuse to play therapist. She needs to learn not to depend on you anymore. She needs to stop thinking about you. Period. The next time she calls, explain that you're making things worse by continuing to console her. She's going to insist it's not true and beg you not to abandon her. Be stern (it'll be hard) and tell her you think the best thing for both of you is not to talk for a while. If she's despondent and you can't bear to cut her off completely, offer to communicate with her via e-mail a couple times a week, but that's it. She's in rehab and, in this case, the drug is you.

I've been dating a woman at work and want to break things off—which won't make her happy. How should I act around her at the office to make this easier for both of us?

Yikes. You've heard what they say about the fury of a woman scorned, haven't you? They're not kidding. Once you break up, you can't really prevent her from leaving roadkill in your in box or telling everyone at work that you're an underendowed creep. But you can maintain your own professionalism by refusing to cause a scene or let the situation get in the way of doing your job well.

So break up with her as gently as possible. Ask her if she still wants to be friendly with you at work or if she'd rather you left her alone for a while. Then respect her wishes—whatever they are. If she tells you to go to hell before you even can ask the question, your best bet is to avoid talking about the split with anyone at work and try like hell to stay out of her way.

Would you prefer a guy to act like a jerk before dumping you so it's easier for you to get over him?

No! But I do have guy friends who use that terrible tactic. The pain and confusion I'd feel if the guy I loved started being mean while we were still dating would be much worse than if he just ended it and left me pining away for the sweetheart I remembered. Besides, like I said in the introduction to this chapter, gaining a reputation as a bastard *will* come back to haunt you.

How can I break up with a girl and manage to stay friends with her? I've been dating this party-girl type for about a year now and it's just not working out. I'm looking for someone more mature. She's just so much fun, though, I'd hate to never see her again.

The secret to staying friends with someone is to be honest, fair, and considerate of her feelings—especially when you're breaking up. If she walks away from this relationship thinking you're fundamentally a good person and someone she's enjoyed spending time with, keeping you as a long-term friend will appeal to her—after she's gotten over the initial sting of rejection.

So start by telling her exactly what you just told me, but replace the word "mature" with the words "ready to settle down" so she doesn't feel slighted. Before you end the breakup conversation, ask her what you can do to help her deal with this—call her every day, stop contacting her completely, check in on her once a month? Then do as she asks. If you haven't cheated, lied, or otherwise mistreated her, the only reason she'd refuse your friendship is because she loves you too much to be with you and not be your girlfriend.

I dumped her and now she won't speak to me. Which is fine, except there's a lot of my stuff in her apartment that I'd like to have back. How should I go about getting it?

If she hasn't already thrown your favorite things out the window or sold them on ebay, reminding her she still possesses a few of these things could be just the nudge she needs to cause their immediate destruction. If a guy who just cruelly tossed me aside called to inquire about his beloved gray sweater, it wouldn't be long for this world. This is standard—not psycho—behavior. So don't assume your otherwise levelheaded ex would never do such a thing.

Why not take the opposite tack? Lie low and wait several weeks. Then send her an e-mail saying you have a few of *her* things she'd probably like, and were hoping she'd return the favor. Suggest meeting outside her place early one weekday evening for a fast exchange, or offer to arrange a FedEx pickup if she never wants to see your face again.

My girlfriend and I were together 5 years before we broke up. I'm really close with her family—especially her little brother. Is there any way I can maintain my relationship with him even though his sister can't stand me?

No. Your only connection with that family is through her. And when you severed ties with her, you lost them, too. Maybe someday in the future if you and your ex manage to reestablish a friendship, you can be buddy-buddy with her bro again. Until then, there's nothing you really can do.

My ex and I started sleeping together again, which I don't mind at all. But I suspect she thinks we might get back together. How can I make it clear that that's not going to happen?

The only way to make it crystal clear is to tell her flat out every time you're with her that you love having sex with her but do *not* want a relationship of any kind. But even then you'll be guilty of sending mixed signals because your mouth will say no while your body says yes. If you can handle the guilt, then party on—she's an adult and responsible for her own emotional well-being. But if you really want to do what's best for her, get out of her bed for good.

■ When You're Dumped

Why do women usually break up with their boyfriends?

After just a few months: Because when the infatuation wears off, we realize you aren't as sexy/exciting/smart/interesting as we thought you were. After a year: Because you haven't been giving us the love and attention we need to be happy, or we feel like we can't trust you—or both. After 2 years: Because we sense you're never going to want to live together/get married. After several years: Because your core values and life philosophies are at odds with ours.

Percentage of people who think most relationships fizzle because of . . .
Lack of effective communication: **53**
Money problems: **29**
Interference of relatives: **7**
Previous relationships: **3**
(SOURCE: Roper Starch Worldwide survey, 1998)

Why do you cry when we break up—even when it's your idea?

Because breakups are sad, and female emotions don't always make sense. When we start dating someone, we secretly hope that he'll be The One. So when another relationship gets kicked to the curb, we can't help but feel heartbroken. We've just been sent back to Go and it sucks. Even though things aren't working out, it doesn't mean we want to forget all the good things. We'll never wake up in your apartment again. Your friends will no longer be our friends. That thing you do that drives us crazy in the sack—what if no other guy knows how to do that? We may have decided to give you up, but we don't want to lose all of you. Irrational? Yes. But true.

My girlfriend says we should see other people. I'm guessing this is a nice way of saying sayonara, and she's got somebody waiting in the wings. Am I right?

The only time I've used that line was when I'd met another guy and wanted to swap body fluids with a clear conscience. But because the guy might a) turn out to be a creep or b) refuse to commit, I wanted to keep the old boyfriend around as backup. Look, even if your girl isn't coveting another man's *cojones*, believe me when I tell you she's definitely toying with the idea of dumping you altogether.

Your best line of defense is to agree to her "see other people" suggestion, then drop the hint a few days later that you've got a hot date lined up. Best-case scenario: She freaks, accuses you of being a cheat and/or scumbag, then hurls your favorite bobble head at you. But when the tantrum's over, she might rethink whether she wants to risk losing you. Worst-case scenario: She smiles and says, "That's great, honey," in which case you know she's already as good as gone.

Six Signs You're About to Get Axed

1. She yells at you just for breathing too loud/walking funny/being tall.
2. She stops calling you pet names.
3. She'd rather party with her friends on the weekend than hang with you.
4. She lets go of your hand every time you try to hold it.
5. She changes the subject when you suggest going on vacation together.
6. She has a stomachache/PMS/headache every time you try to have sex.

Don't beg, wallow, pout, or otherwise act like a pathetic weakling—that sets us on an immediate stud hunt. If you think she's worth reeling back in, act confident and laid-back, wear the clothes she likes on you, and have something out of the ordinary planned every other night of the week—think live Latin jazz and salsa lessons, not Chinese takeout and a rental.

If that doesn't reignite her flame, there's only one way to get out of this sucky situation with your dignity intact: Say sayonara yourself.

She just left me a week ago and she's already dating someone else. Does that mean she was cheating on me?

Probably, but does it really matter either way? She's gone. It's over. The more you think about it, the more pissed you're going to get. Hard as it is, just block out the details. Every time you think about her, force yourself to switch mental tracks. One trick I use to banish bad thoughts is to memorize something—like a list of all the countries in Africa or the capitals of all 50 states, depending on your geographical prowess—and repeat it to myself whenever unwanted thoughts creep in. Get hypnotized if you have to, but get her out of your head.

I keep asking my girlfriend why she's breaking up with me and she won't give me answers. Why doesn't she just tell me?

Remember the scene in the movie *A Few Good Men* when Jack Nicholson lost it? He screamed, "You can't handle the truth!" Well, I'm guessing that's what your girlfriend thinks every time you ask why she's ending things. Her reasons must be hurtful ones—like she's not attracted to or excited by you anymore. Or that she found someone else. If you keep pestering her, she'll probably spit it out. But remember what my friend Liesa always says: Don't ask questions that you really don't want to know the answers to.

Percentage of men who say they've stopped dating someone because a parent disapproved of him or her: **9**
Percentage of women: **14**

(SOURCE: Bruskin Research for Women.com)

She dumped me because her parents don't approve of me. Is there any way I can win her back?

It depends on two things: how much you're willing to work and why her parents didn't like you in the first place. If the reason is fairly superficial, there's always the possibility that if you change, they'll come around. If they think you're a bum who's not good enough for their baby, for instance, you might have to get a college degree, a better job, or whatever else it would take to impress them. If the reason is something like religion or race, you're up against a real monster—and without your girlfriend's help, you face slim odds of overcoming their ignorance. And there's no point in doing *anything* unless you know that your girlfriend will take you back if Mommy and Daddy say it's okay.

My girlfriend of 3 years just broke it off. Last week I hit it off with a great girl I'd love to date—but I'm not exactly over my ex yet. Should I confess that I'm on the rebound and ask her to wait?

Yes, definitely confess. "Hitting it off" with someone doesn't happen every day, and you have nothing to lose. Tell her your situation, stressing how great you think she is and that you'd love to take her out. Then explain that you need some time before you'll be ready to start dating. She'll be flattered and will admire your maturity. Unfortunately, you can't ask her not to see other guys in the meantime (that would be out of line and creepy), so you'll just have to call and e-mail her once in a while and hope she holds out for you. On that note, contact her only when you feel upbeat—you don't want to drone on about your breakup or sound pathetic. In fact, talk about your ex as little as possible. If you're lucky, this chick will still be around when you're fully recovered.

I just got burned by a girl and can't stop thinking about her. I know it's going to take time, but how much time? Is there any way to get over her faster?

Expect to feel like damaged goods for somewhere between 2 and 8 months. In the meantime, sever all contact with your new ex and sweat as much as possible. That's right, sweat. Exercise keeps you focused on something besides your bum luck, causes your body to release all sorts of feel-good hormones, and ensures you'll be exhausted when you hit the pillow at night so you won't lie awake thinking about *her*. Start lifting weights, running, bike riding—any physical activity that simultaneously tuckers you out and buffs your bod. Work out every day like it's your job. By the time your feelings for her have faded, you'll look and feel like a rock star.

If you're not the workout type, sign up for some kind of class and pay for it with the cash you would have spent dating her. Try guitar, Spanish, HTML, oil painting, wine tasting, whatever, and throw yourself into it headfirst. Another great breakup elixir? Travel. Go somewhere exotic, exciting, and unexplored by most tourists, someplace with scenery unlike anything you've ever laid eyes on. (Think Iceland, Peru, Mongolia, the Seychelles.) Don't come back until you've kissed a pretty native.

Looking for a soundtrack for your misery? Break out your iPod and download a few (or all) of these:

"Find Yourself Another Girl" by The Hives

"Femme Fatale" by The Velvet Underground and Nico

"Here Comes My Baby" by Cat Stevens

"I'm Lookin' through You" by The Beatles

"Stupid Girl" by The Rolling Stones

"She Loves Me Not" by Papa Roach

"Shot Down in Flames" by AC/DC

"Song for the Dumped" by Ben Folds Five

"Something I Can Never Have" by Nine Inch Nails

"Whenever You Breathe Out I Breathe In" by Modest Mouse

Why does a woman go back to an ex?

There are plenty of bad reasons— she's lazy, lonely, bored, horny, pathetically afraid she can't do better. But the only good reason is because she's convinced that something crucial about the guy or the relationship has changed, something that makes the reason why they split no longer valid. I know a woman, for instance, who broke up with her college sweetheart after graduation because they each took a job on a different coast. Five years later, when they found themselves living in the same city, they got back together. Good reason. My friend Kelly had broken up with her ex because he said he couldn't handle commitment— they started dating again when he agreed to move in with her.

Good reason. Sometimes it takes a breakup to make people smarten up.

How can I get her to consider dating me again?

First, refer to the previous answer and remember why she dumped you. Then prove to her you're a changed man—that you've eradicated or transformed whatever it was about you that she couldn't live with or love. Next, show her that you are now totally devoted to her and willing to do whatever it takes to make her happy by raising your level of commitment higher than it was before you split. If you were casually dating, for example, tell her you want to see her exclusively. If she was already your girl-friend, tell her you want to move in with her. If you were already living together, ask her to marry you. It's the only way she'll believe you mean business. Finally, shower her with tokens of your newfound feelings. It's totally cliché to send her flowers and buy her gifts—but do it anyway. The more of an effort you make, the better your chances at reconciliation will be.

GIRLS OVERHEARD:
In-Bed Deal Breakers

The Scene

Sprawled in my living room. I invited these girls over for a lasagna dinner with wine. Several bottles into the evening, we're swapping slurred stories about things that turned us off before, during, or after sex to the point that we didn't want to see the guy again.

The Guest List

Carrie, 29, a record company exec and bombshell
Jessica, 28, a fashion designer who just started her own business
Cynthia, 27, a human resources exec at a major corporation

Me: This guy I once dated took me into his bedroom for the first time and there was a stack of hand towels on his bedside table clearly for postsex cleanups. How gross is that? As if that weren't enough, he went to the bathroom with the door open. I hightailed it out of there before he could get his hands on me.

Cynthia: For me, if a guy takes me back to his place and he has a roommate, there's no way I'm hooking up with him.

Jessica: Why not?

Cynthia: Because grown men shouldn't have roommates. End of story.

Carrie: The number-one deal breaker for me is a guy who can't kiss.

Me: If he has bad teeth or bad breath, there won't even be a kiss in the first place.

Carrie: True.

Jessica: Bad breath is a deal breaker if it's really halitosis. I mean, it's one thing if you both just ate Italian food and have temporary garlic breath. It's another thing if he has that sort of indescribable, permanent bad breath that has nothing to do with what he puts in his mouth.

Carrie: It's just bad health. His gums are rotting or something. Doesn't gingivitis give you bad breath?

Cynthia: But beyond breath, Carrie's right. A bad kisser isn't going to have very much luck getting women into bed.

Carrie: Because if he can't kiss right, how could he possibly be good in bed?

Me: So what's the difference between a good and a bad kiss?

Jessica: Okay, a good kiss starts off slow and gentle. Then your lips open and you start a little tongue contact. You only go into make-out mode after the gentle stuff. A bad kiss is wet and sloppy right out of the gate. He opens his mouth too wide, sticks his tongue too far into your mouth, and presses against your face too hard.

Carrie: A good kiss is one that's in sync. He has to respond to the way you kiss, not just do what he always does with every girl.

Me: What are some other sexual deal breakers?

Jessica: If he smells. I was hooking up with a guy the other night and when he took his shirt off, I got a wave of B.O. that made my eyes water. It was a really hot night, but still. By this point in his life, he should have discovered a functional deodorant. I couldn't get turned on because it was so foul.

Cynthia: If a guy refuses to use a condom, he's out.

Carrie: Oh, yeah. Of course.

Jessica: Absolutely.

Carrie: Here's another hygiene thing. If a guy uses baby powder in his crotch, that really freaks me out. It just doesn't feel right to be with a man who smells like a toddler. I understand the chafing thing and all that, but save the powder for when you're not looking to make an impression.

Jessica: What if a guy has dirt under his nails?

Cynthia: Yuck.

Me: What if a guy is a little too rough the first time you sleep with him? Like he pinches your nipples or grabs your butt kind of hard. That not only turns me off; it scares me. I'll change my phone number to make sure he never calls again.

Jessica: Yeah, that's frightening. It's one thing if you've been dating for a while and want to play dirty, but not on the first night—he'd seem like a psychopath or an S&M nut job.

Carrie: Here's a great one: hickeys. Men who so much as attempt to leave a mark on my body are immediately asked to leave.

Cynthia: I'll back that up.

Jessica: I've been holding this one back. The single biggest sex deal breaker for me is when a guy pushes on the back of my head during oral sex.

Carrie: That is the most degrading, horrible thing. Oh, here's something even worse. I was with a guy who suddenly— and vigorously—tried for anal sex, and when I pulled away and asked him what he was doing, he claimed that it "accidentally" slipped into the wrong hole.

Jessica: What a creep! Did you ever see him again?

Carrie: What do you think?

7

NOW IT'S
GETTING SERIOUS

**Some Smallish Stuff ■ Major Issues ■
Good Fun, Great Gifts, Hot Sex
■ The Ex, Jealousy, and Cheating** (or Not)
■ Taking the Next Step (or Not)

I get the feeling you guys don't make a conscious decision to be in a serious relationship. You just wake up one morning next to a woman and realize you have tampons under your bathroom sink and *Runaway Bride* in your DVD player, and the last time you did laundry, you noticed a suspicious number of thong panties clinging to your socks.

Despite this, you're always taken by surprise when we want to have The Talk. I'm convinced that if women never brought up commitment, guys would still be faithful, attentive, supportive boyfriends—just a lot less skittish about the whole thing. Unfortunately, our security-seeking instincts kick in after a few months and we need to know that you feel the same about us as we do about you and that—until breakup do us part—you are officially off the market.

Once you're a "couple," everything is pretty much the same as it was before—yet totally different. You'll soon discover that your girlfriend has about 100 different moods, 1,000 ways to express them, and all sorts of wild expectations about what a good boyfriend says and does. The good news is that because you're officially her boyfriend now, the girl you're dating will try even harder to keep you happy. She'll bake you cookies for no reason, give you back massages in bed, and be your biggest fan whether you're climbing the corporate ladder or playing pickup basketball. All in all she'll make your life a whole lot better. But, by nature, relationships are complicated and tricky to maintain. So I'm not surprised you have so many questions about how to make them work over the long haul. These answers will help you to stay together—and stay sane.

■ Some Smallish Stuff

How many nights a week do you expect to spend with your boyfriend? I'm really busy these days but don't want to short-change the woman I'm seeing.

> It's hard to say exactly. Maybe 3 to 5? Some weeks I could spend every waking moment with the guy I'm dating, and other weeks I get claustrophobic and need to be alone or hang with my friends. It's probably best if you see your girlfriend only when you sincerely want to. Otherwise, you'll start to resent her because you don't have time to do everything else you want to do—like go to the gym, read a book, play basketball, or just stay home and watch the History Channel. Thanks to the late-night booty call, I've discovered you can do everything else and maintain a serious relationship at the same time. There's something about falling asleep and waking up together that makes you feel connected as a couple even if you're going on dates only 2 or 3 times a week.

My girlfriend and I spend a lot of time at her apartment, but I'm allergic to her stupid cat. Can I ask her to ditch it?

> No. People and their cats are weirdly attached. They talk about and treat them like they're children. So it would be like asking her to give her baby the boot. But because the thing makes you physically ill, you have every right to limit the amount of time

you spend at her place. When you are there, take allergy medication in her presence so she knows you're making an effort to cope. Down the line, should you ever decide to move in together, she's going to have to decide if her cat's company is more important than your comfort.

After dates, we always end up back at my girlfriend's place because that's what she prefers. Why is she so bent on sleeping in her bed, and how can I make her more willing and eager to come to mine?

Ever notice how many products your girlfriend uses in the morning? Right. So you know they couldn't possibly fit in the cute little purse she brings with her at night. That means if she's like most women and she wants to look and feel like herself the next day, you have to crash at her place. And if she wore high heels and a flashy outfit on Saturday night, she'll feel pretty uncomfortable wearing the same thing at Sunday brunch.

To alleviate the problem, empty a drawer or shelf for her and invite her to bring over a few outfits. Buy her brand of shampoo and conditioner for the shower. If she wears contacts, keep a bottle of saline solution around. If you want to go overboard (and make her feel like the luckiest girl on earth),

Percentage of female college students who expect a boyfriend to . . .

Be sexually faithful: **99**

Continue to see her even if she didn't want to have sex: **98**

Introduce her as your girlfriend: **95**

Introduce her to your family: **94**

Take care of her when she's sick: **90**

Hold her hand in public: **79**

Send her flowers on special occasions: **73**

Carry heavy things for her: **66**

Tell her you love her: **66**

Call her pet names: **39**

(SOURCE: *Hooking Up, Hanging Out, and Hoping for Mr. Right: College Women on Mating and Dating Today*, an Institute for American Values Report to the Independent Women's Forum)

buy her some slippers and serve her favorite kind of coffee or tea in the morning.

My girlfriend really likes to cook, but she's not that good at it. I don't want to hurt her feelings, but I also don't want to eat her food. What can I do?

Buy her a very simple cookbook with recipes you like and give it to her as a gift. She'll think it's so sweet that you bought it for her, she won't even consider an ulterior motive. If you can spare the cash, buy her cooking lessons for her next birthday or your anniversary. In the meantime, hold your nose and swallow.

My girlfriend of 2 years has put on a little weight recently—I'd say 10 to 15 pounds. She eats too many unhealthy things and hasn't been exercising as much as she used to. When I mention it, she claims I should love her no matter how she looks. Can I get her to lead a healthier lifestyle? Or am I being shallow?

You're afraid your girlfriend is heading down the slippery slope to Chubsville—a perfectly valid concern. Valid or not, bringing up her newly formed flab will only make her feel unattractive and less confident—two emotions that lead straight to the bottom of a bag of chips. Instead, stock up on fresh fruit and good-for-you snacks. If she's truly in a lazy, gluttonous stage, she'll eat whatever's in sight. Then ask her to do active things with you like snowboarding, ice-skating, or racquetball. (Avoid words like "workout," "gym," and "fatass.") If you suggest game-like activities, it takes the emphasis off weight control and sounds like you just want to have a good time with her. If she's always enjoyed being active and fit, she'll suddenly remember how good it feels to break a sweat and will probably regain her healthy attitude in no time.

I love my girlfriend and we get along great, but she freaks me out when she has PMS. She says she just gets emotional some-times and everything irritates her. Does she want me around, or should I lie low for a few days?

If she's like most women, she'd probably prefer that you stick around and suck it up. Women bleed from their crotch every

28 days, for crissake! We have to stuff wads of dry cotton into our most sensitive orifices and then extract them later by yanking on a string. Can you think of an equivalent nuisance men have to deal with on a monthly basis? No. PMS usually lasts only a few days, so cut your woman some slack. Stay by her side and let her nastiness roll off of you like raindrops on a weatherproof deck. Here's a tip to make that easier: Back her up no matter what the ridiculous thing is she's complaining about—she's much less likely to swing at you if she thinks you're in her corner.

How can I help my girlfriend relax when she's stressed-out?

Let her yap. Women need to talk things through to feel like we have a handle on a situation. So even if you don't feel like hearing the details, ask her to tell you all about it. As her tirade subsides, walk up behind her and start rubbing her shoulders and neck. Suggest that she lie down and let you give her a proper massage. (And if the massage takes a sexual turn, that's a good thing for her, too—sex is very relaxing.) If she doesn't react well to your hands-on technique, she could be too jittery to stay still, in which case suggest going for a walk or a run together to let off some steam.

Percentage of women who calm themselves down by . . .
Talking to someone: **38**
Thinking about what's bothering them: **29**
Exercising: **13**
Eating: **5**
Having sex: **2**
Having a drink: **2**

(SOURCE: *USA Today*, October 9, 2000)

If I express my desire for my fiancée to get a Brazilian bikini wax, what are the chances she'll be into it?

The problem with said request is that your fiancée will assume you think she's not up to snuff as is and you'd prefer her privates to resemble those of a porn star, or a child for that matter. (She's also bound to wonder where you got the bright idea, which could lead to big trouble.) If you think she can handle that without being insulted or hurt, go ahead and suggest a trim. But first, take a moment to imagine yourself lying on your back with your ankles behind your ears, having your curlies ripped violently from your crotch in one agonizing yank. Would you be willing to take one for the team?

When is it okay to fart in front of someone you've been dating awhile?

Under no circumstances should you pass wind before reaching Relationship Comfort Level 5. In order to get to Comfort Level 5 with your girlfriend, you have to pass Levels 1 through 4. Level 1: Belching for longer than 3 seconds midconversation. Level 2: Scratching your crotch/butt crack while in her direct line of sight. Level 3: Taking a whiz while she's in the shower. Level 4: Announcing you're about to take a dump. If she doesn't leave you after witnessing those delights, go ahead and turn on the gas.

My girlfriend is self-conscious about her small breasts. I love them. How do I get her to feel more comfortable with her body?

Giving her hot little A-cups lots and lots of loving attention will definitely help, but you're probably already doing that just by touching and kissing them during sex. Reinforce the hands-on appreciation with comments like "You have the most beautiful/ perfect/sexy breasts." She may be worried that you secretly wish she had more up front, and sincere, enthusiastic praise will convince her otherwise. On that note, if she catches you checking out busty babes on the street, it will just add fuel to her big-boobs-are-better fire, so try to keep your eyes in check. But that's really all you can do—be positive and don't send mixed signals. Body-image problems are a very personal issue. Being a fan of her figure can kick-start her confidence, but she'll have to take it from there.

So many women wear too much makeup, including my girlfriend. How do I tell her?

You can't tell her she wears too much makeup without starting a fight that's bound to end in long black streaks of mascara running down her heavily powdered cheeks. What you can do is encourage her to ease up on the Cover Girl by mentioning how naturally gorgeous she looks first thing in the morning or right after she gets out of the shower. Make it a habit to praise her looks whenever she happens to be fresh-faced. Women pay careful attention to compliments from the man they're crazy about: Tell us you love the way we smell and we'll wear that perfume every time we see you; mention how sexy our hair looks when we wear it up and suddenly it's all ponytails and French braids. It's one way of showing that we want to make you happy. Anyway, you'll probably be surprised at how quickly she pares down her beauty routine, or at least switches to products that contain the word "natural" in their name.

Percentage of women worldwide who agree that beauty products are a necessity, not a luxury: **82**

(SOURCE: Avon Global Women's Survey 2000)

There's this thing my girlfriend does that drives me crazy. She'll complain that I don't do something—like buy her flowers, call to see if she got home safely, or take her to nice restaurants. Then when I do them, she accuses me of only doing it because she wants me to. How can I get her to see she's being unfair?

Oh, yeah. I know this phenomenon. I've been guilty of it myself. Your girlfriend is miffed because she wishes you were the kind of guy who would do these things of his own accord—but you're not. So she doesn't appreciate the flowers, the phone call, or the fancy night out because she considers them insincere. After all, it's the thought that counts and in this case it was *her* thought, not yours.

The point she's missing is that you sincerely want to make her happy. So emphasize the other ways that you show her you care—ways she may not notice because they don't mesh with her notions of romance (which sound pretty stereotypical). If you want to play her game, when she complains that you haven't brought her flowers, don't bring her flowers—bring her a new CD. When she complains that you don't buy her jewelry, don't buy her jewelry—buy her flowers. It may seem ridiculous, but I bet it'll make her happy.

I smoke and my girlfriend wants me to quit. I don't want to quit and don't plan to. How can I get her to stop bugging me about it?

Sorry to have to tell you this, but she's never going to stop bugging you about it. Never. She's doing it for your benefit—to keep your lungs from turning black and cancerous, to keep your teeth from falling out, to keep your penis from going limp (smoking can lead to impotence, in case you didn't know). The health hazards of secondhand smoke affect her life every time she sees you, not to mention the ubiquitous smell and taste of nicotine. Maybe if you promised not to smoke around her, switched to a lower-tar brand, and/or agreed to cut back, she would back off a little. But as long as you continue smoking, she'll continue bitching.

Percentage of women who think couples fight most about the following issues . . .
Money: **37**
Jealousy: **35**
How to spend free time: **11**
Chores: **7**
Planning (from vacations to marriage): **3**
Fidelity: **3**
Sex: **3**
Family: **1**
(SOURCE: about.com dating survey)

My girlfriend constantly stumps me with such questions as "Do I look fat?" and "Do you think she's pretty?" I never get the answers right. What should I say?

A woman asks questions like these only if she already knows that the true answer to both is "Yes." If she were content with the truth, she wouldn't ask in the first place. What she wants is a little white lie that will help her sleep easier at night. So the correct answer to the fat question is "No. How could you possibly look fat when you're not?" The correct answer to the pretty question is "I guess. But she's not as pretty as you." Tacking on a sincere "You'll always be the most beautiful woman to me" may feel as corny as hell, but it'll make her insecurities melt faster than a Popsicle in the sun.

■ Major Issues

We fight a lot, about everything from who left the car door unlocked to what movie we should rent, but when we're not fighting we get along great. Are we just not right for each other?

These sound like harmless sibling-style spats. As a matter or fact, toss a few lighthearted jokes and some playful groping into the mix and they start to look a lot like flirting. Even if your fights sometimes ruin a good time and upset one or both of you, it doesn't mean you're not right for each other. It just means you suck at communicating differences of opinion. Try this: When an argument starts, nip it in the bud by refusing to fight. Not easy, I know, but not as hard as you might think. Just remember that by not fighting you're actually winning. If you think it's more than small-time squabbles, go to a couples therapist. People do it all the time and say it really works.

My girlfriend doesn't drink often, but when she does, there's a one-in-three chance she's going to get angry and pick a fight with me. She knows it happens and always apologizes about it the next day, but she still does it. Is it fair for me to ask her to stop drinking?

It's fair for you to ask her to stop drinking—when she's around you. Or you can refuse to be around her when she drinks.

How can I make a good impression with her parents?

I asked my mother and the first words out of her mouth were "Put on a clean shirt." But it's more complicated than that. If you're going to her parents' house, taking a gift of wine or dessert or flowers is essential—and expected. To really impress, send a brief

DEFUSE FEMALE FURY
Your Five-Point Plan

1. **Don't try to rationalize with an enraged woman.** Let her cry, shout, accuse, and/or throw things, without interruption. Save any self-defensive comments or denials for later, when she's actually listening. Right now, she's the Hulk and the only thing you can do is wait until she turns back into David Banner.

2. **Use defusing language.** As she starts to calm down, comfort her (without incriminating yourself) by telling her you're sorry she's upset, you're sorry you did whatever it was you did because obviously it really hurt her. Tell her you care about her and want to resolve this.

3. **Repaint the scene from your point of view.** Don't tell her she's wrong; just tell your side of the story, explaining why you did the things you did. She's going to interrupt you often to criticize this or that action or assumption—

but sincere thank-you card a couple of days later. Parents also watch to see how you treat their daughter. Do you listen to her without interrupting? Do you ask her opinions? Physical closeness is okay—it should be obvious that you're comfortable with each other—but excessive displays of affection get a thumbs-down. "It shows you don't respect her parents," says Mom.

My mother and my girlfriend don't get along. My mother doesn't think my girlfriend is good enough for me. My girlfriend thinks my mom is controlling and bitchy. How can I end the feud?

Yikes! You've got to hope that each loves you enough to cut the other some slack. To get them to do this, you have to use the right approach. Don't take sides. Don't defend one to the other. Don't ask them to ease up by saying their opinions about the so let her. But don't take the bait; just continue explaining your point of view.

4. Own up. If you did something insensitive or inconsiderate, admit it and let her know you'll try to avoid doing it again in the future. If you really feel like you did nothing wrong, get into the fundamentals of the issue when she's calm enough to handle a rational debate. It may be that you have to agree to disagree.

5. Get physical. Now that she's calm, put your arm around her and kiss her. Silently remind her that receiving affection and physical comfort/pleasure from each other is one of the reasons you both put up with a relationship. If kissing turns into making out, which turns into makeup sex, this fight is officially over.

other person are wrong. Just ask each of them if they could please, for your sake, try to overlook the negative qualities they perceive in the other person. Tell them how happy it would make you if they would be a little nicer to each other. Frankly, it sounds like they both need to be reminded that loving someone means being willing to make sacrifices.

Last night my girlfriend started crying and telling me that I don't give her enough attention. We hang out at least three or four times a week, and talk on the phone or via e-mail every day we don't. What else does she want?

Women pay close attention to such details as who is calling whom, who is e-mailing whom. If she feels like she's always calling or e-mailing you first, she just may want you to initiate contact more often. Quantity is more important than quality here, so if you have absolutely nothing to say, cheat by e-mailing her a news article that might interest her or something silly from a humor Web site, like theonion.com. Sing a song on her answering machine, call her to tell her what you had for lunch, whatever—she'll just be glad to hear from you.

Then, when you're with her, ask her how she's feeling and you'll earn major points. A little physical affection will make her feel like your number-one concern even if you're focusing 100 percent of your mental attention on the TV, so hold her hand or put your arm around her more than usual. This may sound like a lot of work, but trust me, there's a big payoff: A girlfriend who feels like she's totally appreciated will stop worrying about what *she* wants and start focusing her time and energy on making *you* the happiest guy on earth.

I love the fact that my girlfriend and I are so different, but sometimes it really gets in the way. Basically I'm extroverted and she's introverted. I like to go out, see a lot of people, party. She'd rather stay home or go out to dinner with just one other couple. Is this relationship going to work?

Of course it's going to work—as long as neither of you expects the other to change. If you want to continue doing things together, you'll have to spend a few more nights at home than you'd like, and she'll have to spend a few more nights out. And sometimes you'll just have to go your separate ways and be okay with that. I've been in this situation before, and one great way to deal with it is for you to go to parties early and have your girlfriend meet you out an hour or two later. That way she gets a smaller dose of socializing. You could also leave parties a little early to get home and watch the second half of a movie with her. Compromise, baby. That's what it's all about.

I'm in a long-distance relationship with a great girl, but since we only see each other two or three weekends a month, how do

I know whether or not we'd actually get along if we lived in the same town and saw each other all the time?

A good way to put your everyday compatibility to the test is to take a long vacation together that involves some logistics and adventure. Think camping. Think road trip. Think a very foreign country. Setting yourselves up for a few challenges will test how well you work together as a team and whether you can stand each other's crappier qualities—which are sure to come out some night when you're tired, hungry, and lost. If you make it through even the toughest situations and still want to make out at the end of the day, the odds that you'll get along if you lived closer to each other are pretty high.

We're going on our first 2-week vacation together and I want it to go really well. Is there anything I can do to up the chances that we won't fight or get annoyed with each other?

Yes. First of all, do some research. Vacations get stressful when you get to your destination and have no idea how to get around, where to find a good hotel or restaurant, or what to do for fun. If you have options in mind all the time, then things will go a lot more smoothly. Second, if you'll be roughing it by camping, driving/flying overnight, or doing any number of strenuous, dirty activities, make sure you schedule in some R&R for the day after—somewhere you can take showers, eat good food, and lounge around comfortably. Enough rest, food, and pampering is crucial for good relations. Also, know what she doesn't like. If she usually complains about crowds and traffic, don't go to Mexico City. If she gets bored and antsy sitting in one place for too long, don't go to a secluded beach. Last, attitude is everything. Being psyched to be there with her and showing it will make her happy no matter where you are.

My girlfriend is obsessed with dieting and working out. Not only am I worried that she has some kind of mental issues, but I'm sick to death of hearing her stress about calories, fat-to-muscle

ratios, and how horrible she feels because she missed one aerobics class. What can I do?

Well, that depends. If she's healthy enough, just preoccupied with food and fitness, there isn't much you can do besides change the subject when it comes up.

If you think she's working out and dieting in dangerous ways, ask yourself: Is her weight healthy, or are her hipbones so sharp they wear out the weave of her Levi's? Does she get the nutrition she needs (signs she's not include dry, sallow skin; acne; and thin, brittle hair)? Does her obsession make her unhappy with herself, frustrated, tired, and irritable? If you answer yes to any of these questions, you may want to suggest she see a therapist. If you don't think she'll listen to you, get her family and friends involved and do it intervention-style.

We've been dating exclusively for almost a year and I really want my girlfriend to go on the Pill. How do I talk to her about it?

Going on the Pill is a big deal. It can make us fat; it can make us crazy. And unless we trust a man 100 percent, not using condoms can feel like playing the STD version of Russian roulette. The best way to broach the subject is to ask her if she's ever thought about going on the Pill and, if so, what her opinions are. Then, before she can answer, quickly add that if she thinks it's too soon to talk about it, you'll understand. The less pressure you put on her, the more likely she'll respond the way you want.

■ Good Fun, Great Gifts, Hot Sex

How can you keep a long-term relationship interesting/exciting?

Remember this: Routine is your enemy. So be unpredictable—from how you have sex to where you go on Saturday nights to what you talk about over dinner. Go see documentaries on controversial topics and hash out how you feel about the issue. Challenge each other to try new things, even if it's something small like ceviche. Show up at her place on a Sunday afternoon driving a convertible you rented just for the day. Ask her questions you've never asked her before. Go to the park and do forward rolls like you did when you were a kid. Get your tarot cards read on the street. Just because you're with the same person doesn't mean anything else has to be the same all the time. And if you constantly come up with great ideas, you'll inspire your girlfriend to do the same.

What are some romantic things a guy has done for you?

Baked me a cake on my birthday. Took me to an outdoor concert and made out with me while lying on the grass. Bought a Web address that was a combination of our names. Called me from the plane to tell me how much he was going to miss me. Watched me sleeping and then told me he loved me the minute I woke up. Kissed away my tears. Picked me up and carried me down the street. Gave me a foot massage after I had worn stiletto heels all night to turn him on. Told me I looked incredibly sexy bundled up in a hat, scarf, and winter coat.

What are the gifts women want most?

Without a doubt, jewelry. Even if you're dating the crunchiest, hippiest girl around, she'll still melt over a crystal hanging from a leather choker the same way a more high-maintenance chick will die for a charm bracelet from Tiffany's. And the fact that we know you don't understand or share our fixation for pretty things that dangle from our necks, ears, and wrists makes the gift even more thoughtful.

What kind of flowers besides a dozen red roses (too predictable) will make her swoon?

1. 10 giant yellow sunflowers
2. 20 pink French tulips
3. 15 fire-red gerber daisies

I'm planning to buy my girlfriend jewelry for Christmas, but I'm not sure what to get. She has a simple style—one of the things I love about her—so she probably won't like anything big or flashy. We've been dating for 2 years. Any suggestions?

My pick: a pair of tiny diamond stud earrings. She'll wear them every day. If diamonds seem too symbolic for you, get her a thin necklace (silver or gold, based upon which she wears more often) with a small jewel pendant. Think pearl if she's old-fashioned or romantic, black jade if she's exotic or sophisticated, ruby if she's feisty or sexy, or cat's-eye if she's outdoorsy or rebellious. Whatever you do, don't buy her a watch—that's what her dad is buying her mom for their 35th wedding anniversary, not what she wants from you.

How can I make a special-occasion dinner more special?

Make reservations at the kind of restaurant she can wear a little black dress to (the cheapest entrée on the menu should be $16). Send flowers to her office or home that day with a card that says something along the lines of "Can't wait to see you tonight." She'll love that. Pick her up on time dressed as well as you know how. Compliment everything about her, hold her hand during dinner, and bring up sexy and/or funny memories. Try to keep the conversation away from anything too serious or banal. Talk about a trip you want to take with her in the future. Order a bottle of champagne with dessert, and don't leave until she's tipsy. Then take her home and start kissing her before you reach the door.

Percentage of people who consider the following foods the most sensual . . .
Champagne and wine: **34**
Strawberries: **29**
Chocolate: **23**
Whipped cream: **19**
(SOURCE: Revlon survey of 1,000 people)

Without being kinky and excluding positions, do you have any ideas for how to make lovemaking more exciting to both my girlfriend and me?

The secret to long-term lust is spontaneity—so stay out of the bedroom and take her by surprise. Walk up behind her in the kitchen and start massaging her breasts and kissing her neck—that episode should end up on the kitchen table. Slide your hand between her legs while she's walking up the stairs or brushing her teeth. Watch a scary-as-hell movie to get your adrenaline flowing, then channel the energy into a quickie. Visiting parents also has a way of bringing out the horny teen in all of us. Or go out and get rippin' drunk, then have sloppy sex on the living room floor. Take her dancing and turn it into a hip-grinding tease. Wrestle until you're breathless and sweaty, then start making out hard. Invade her morning shower with the most salacious intentions. Hmmm . . . what else? Oh, yeah, rub massage oil all over her body, then start an X-rated slip-and-slide.

Percentage of women who love to have sex on or in . . .

Front of a fireplace: **61**
A bed-and-breakfast: **52**
A first-class hotel: **47**
A hot tub: **46**
The outdoors: **39**
The shower: **35**
The sofa: **23**
The floor: **17**
A car or truck: **12**
A motel: **7**

(SOURCE: *What Women Want*)

I saw a Victoria's Secret bag around the house, so I figure my girlfriend is going to show up on Valentine's night in some kind of special lingerie. What does she want me to say or do when I see her?

She wants you to say, "Wow," in a low, thick voice and to immediately not be able to keep your hands off her. To cover your butt, drop a line like "You're always beautiful and sexy, but this looks great on you." That way she knows you're really attracted to her, not the garter belt. Be sure to go slow since she'll feel like she wasted 100 bucks if you rip off whatever it is right away. As a matter of fact, try to keep as much of her getup on as possible. Gently tug the fabric down to get at her breasts, and pull the crotch of her panties aside to get at her . . . crotch. On this night, we want sex to be slow and romantic, so the longer you take to get us buck naked, the better.

My fiancée and I have been together more than a year. Before me, her sex life was limited. While I'm no Don Juan, I've been around. Any idea how I can get her to try new things without coming across like a wannabe porn star and freaking her out?

Hmm—you don't mention what, exactly, it is you'd like to try, but I have a hunch the answer is . . . everything. And why shouldn't it be? You're about to enter a lifelong relationship with this woman, so it's natural to want all the excitement and variety possible (short of anything that lands you in the ER or the back-seat of a squad car). There's a very good chance that your bride-to-be wants the same thing. That said, getting her to engage in a sex act more risqué than anything she's ever read in *Cosmo* is going to take some sensitivity and patience. Make it clear you love everything about making love to her—including all the sights, sounds, smells, and tastes—so she realizes there's nothing she should be shy or nervous about. I know it's sappy, but saying things like "I love everything about your body" and "I want us to make each other feel good in as many ways as possible" is a good way to start. When a woman feels safe and loved in a relationship, as your fiancée probably does with you, she's more willing to experiment. Instead of having a clinical conversation about it in advance, which might freak her out, slowly introduce the idea physically. And I mean *slowly*! You want to give her a hint about what it is you'd like to try and then back off to see how she responds. When each small, nonthreatening step feels good and is fun for her, she'll eventually want it to go all the way—whatever "it" is. Just start with the tame stuff and work up to all things kinky.

My girlfriend and I occasionally watch a porno together. She told me the girl-on-girl scenes turn her on the most. Is this normal? Should I be worried that she's a lesbian? Or should I start dropping hints that she get one of her gal pals to join us?

Whoa, slow down! Do *not* drop hints that you're gung ho for a threesome unless you want to get slapped straight back to singledom. Your girlfriend's interest in girl-on-girl stuff doesn't mean she wants same-sex action in reality. It's simply a matter of call and response. Let me explain: Growing up, we women watched the same TV you and your guy friends did. We snuck peeks at the same dirty magazines and stayed up late watching adult flicks on cable. And in each of those media, it was—and still is—the female body presented as the sexually charged one. Just like you did, we learned to associate two-dimensional images of women flashing their tits and bending over with what's supposed to be a turn-on. And, as you already know, two naked female bodies are twice as nice. But impersonal porn has little to do with real-life sex and love. When it comes to flesh and blood, all the brainwashing goes by the wayside and our natural sexual desire for a hairy chest, rough hands, and, um, male anatomy reigns supreme.

> These five seemingly innocent films were declared most likely to get a woman in the mood. Put on a pair of clean boxers, cuddle up on the couch, and press play.
> 1. *Bull Durham*
> 2. *The Mask of Zorro*
> 3. *Henry and June*
> 4. *The Thomas Crown Affair*
> 5. *The Piano*
> (SOURCE: *Men's Health* magazine, May 2002)

What can I do to get my girlfriend to initiate sex more often?

Stop initiating it yourself. On a night when you would usually end up in bed, keep your hands to yourself, but make a point of telling her that she looks incredibly sexy. A funny thing about female arousal is that the sexier you think we are, the sexier we feel. Throw her a few furtive glances and make a comment about how rockin' her various body parts are and she should be snuggling up to you in no time. If you don't want to exert any effort at all, then just don't hit on her for several nights in a row. Eventually she'll get horny and come calling.

How can I get my girlfriend to talk more in bed, tell me what she wants/likes, or just plain talk dirty?

This is a situation where you have to lead by example, and you don't want to come out of the gate using four-letter words or cliché porn questions like "You like this, baby?" One sexy way to introduce erotic chitchat is to ask permission to do things to her.

Percentage of women who talk dirty during sex: **74**

(SOURCE: *Men's Health* magazine, May 2002)

Questions like "Can I take your clothes off?" "Can I touch you here?" "What about here?" will help get her talking. So will asking her how things feel and whether she wants you to go faster or slower. Use a soft, sexy whisper and say her name a lot. Some other things we like to hear that might elicit a response: "I can't wait to be inside you." "I love the way you taste." "You're so wet." Telling her when you're about to come will also encourage her to tell you when she is, which is a huge help if your goal is simultaneous orgasm.

■ The Ex, Jealousy, and Cheating (or Not)

Every time I start dating a new woman, she asks how many women I've slept with in the past. Does she really need (or want) to know? I feel like any number is the wrong answer.

Here's something you may not realize: Women who have slept with more than a dozen or so men seldom, if ever, ask that question. They don't ask it because they don't want to answer it. So if your girl is crunching numbers, it's probably because hers is low. Refusing to answer will only make you look like the gigolo Little Miss Goody-Two-Shoes fears you may be. Be truthful, but realize high numbers might freak her out. I think the magic she'll-be-OK-with-it number is 10—that covers a good four or five serious girlfriends starting from high school and ending with your ex, plus a one-night stand, one friend you fooled around with, one vacation fling, one older-woman type, and one wild card. If your answer is much closer to 20 or more, I suggest simply blowing off the question with a joke, like "Do vegetables count? What about pets?" or "Well, let's see, there's you, your mom, my kindergarten teacher. . . ."

I'm still friends with most of my ex-girlfriends, so I hang out with them occasionally. Every time I do, my girlfriend and I fight about it. She doesn't think I still should see them. How can I make her understand they aren't a threat to her?

Make them her friends. It's the only way she'll ever be comfortable with them—if at all. But if she meets them and sees that your relationship with each of them is totally platonic (being extra affectionate with your girlfriend when an ex is around will only help your cause), her jealousy will eventually subside enough so you won't fight about it anymore. Yes, your girlfriend will have to accept these women as your friends and learn to deal with it, but you'll have to accept that she's threatened by them (regardless of whether she should be) and be considerate of her feelings. And make sure you give her all the time and attention she needs before you dole it out to any other woman—especially an ex.

My girlfriend keeps bugging me about going to Paris with her. It's her favorite city, and she once took a romantic trip there with another guy. I don't care that she's been there with someone else, but why should I have to go there, too? Doesn't she see that it is very unromantic to be put in that situation? Help!

You're right. Reenacting the highlights of your girlfriend's past relationships is anything but romantic. And my first thought was that she's being insensitive. But, after an enlightening discussion with my buddy Liesa, two factors changed my mind: 1) Your girlfriend isn't going to stop loving Paris, so refusing to fly to her favorite city will only make her resent you, and 2) if you don't go, her fondest memories of those places will forever include this other guy. So the only way to win is to show her an all-out amazing time there. Think of it as a memory-replacement mission—out with her loser ex and in with you.

What do I do with pictures of my old girlfriends and letters and stuff? My live-in girlfriend has demanded that I trash them, but I know it'll be fun to look through them when I'm 80.

You could hash it out with your girlfriend, but why not just ask a relative if you can leave a box of stuff in his or her basement?

My fiancée is the super-jealous type. How do I get her to chill?

According to every self-help book and psychologist I've ever consulted, romantic jealousy is usually the result of two things: 1) low self-esteem—she has such a poor image of herself that she can't believe you could be satisfied and happy with just her, and 2) fear of loss—she's so afraid of being hurt she tries to prevent it by policing you.

If she talks a lot about how pretty, smart, or talented other women are, it's probably a self-esteem thing. If her jealousy spreads to anybody and everything else you give your time/attention to, she's likely afraid she'll lose you. In either case, let her know she's being unfair to you. If you've been faithful, tell her you love her but she's going to have to change to make the relationship work. Once she knows she could lose you if she doesn't beat her jealousy, she'll be motivated to change.

To help her get over the green-eyed monster, compliment her on the things that make her a one-of-a-kind human being (the birthmark on her left thigh, the way she laughs, how she touches you, her smell, her bizarre sense of humor, the way she kisses . . . anything unique). The more irreplaceable and loved-for-exactly-who-she-is she feels, the more secure and less jealous she's likely to be.

My girlfriend is kind of flirty with other guys (even in front of me). I don't think she means anything by it—she's really friendly—but how do I know for sure?

If your girlfriend has always been the flirty type, you can be confident it has nothing to do with her devotion to you. Very early in life women learn that flirting is a way of interacting with men that easily earns them a positive response. So for a lot of women, flirting is simply their social M.O. when it comes to men. It becomes a meaningless, if ditzy, habit. I know a happily married Southern-belle type named Rachel who never says a word to a man or boy without tilting her head, raising her voice an octave, and flashing a little-girl smile. Gretchen, a New York–born friend of mine, frequently slips sexual innuendo into her conversations with guys she wouldn't sleep with even if they were the last man on earth. Maybe Rachel, Gretchen, and your girlfriend are conscious of what they're doing—and maybe they aren't. If you don't feel she's disrespecting you in any way, chalk it up to friendliness and ignore it.

My girlfriend is weirdly jealous of my dog, who has never really warmed up to her. If I take it to the park without her, she flips out and says I'd rather be with the dog than her. Is she crazy?

I don't know if she's crazy, but unless you're having sex with it and taking it out to dinner, she definitely shouldn't be jealous of your dog. Obviously, she takes your relationship with it a little too seriously, so I would try to make her lighten up about it by turning it into a joke. Here's an idea: Buy a cheap locket, put a picture of her in it, and make a show of hanging it around the dog's neck. Send flowers to her office and sign your dog's name to the card. Of course, that could make her hate the thing even more—you never know with crazy women.

One of her friends hit on me. Should I tell my girlfriend? Or do I just tell the friend to back off and spare my girlfriend the pain?

I would want my boyfriend to tell me, even though it can only lead to an ugly confrontation. Wouldn't you?

I cheated. Should I tell her?

Here's something I've learned about cheating: Every time a friend—male or female—has gotten some on the side, it was because they weren't blown away by the person they were with and/or the relationship wasn't an honest or satisfying one—and, because of that, things would have ended whether they 'fessed up or not. So take the fact that you've cheated as a sure sign that something is very wrong with your relationship. If you want things to be right, think about why you strayed and, yes, talk to her about it—even though it will be pure hell. Otherwise, keep the bad news to yourself, break up with her, and find someone you actually want to be committed to.

Percentage of men who have cheated on a partner at some point in their lives: **55**
Percentage of women: **59**

(SOURCE: *Cosmopolitan* magazine, May 2002)

Have you or your friends cheated on their significant others? What makes a girlfriend stray?

With our current significant others? No. But I can't say it hasn't happened in the past. Women often cheat when they feel unappreciated and neglected by the person they're seeing. They want to confirm that they're still attractive, so they look for the attention elsewhere. I've noticed that it's women with low self-esteem who end up in other guys' beds the most. If your girlfriend is confident, she won't doubt that she can get laid whenever she wants, so she won't need to prove it. Instead, she'll just confront you about the fact that she isn't satisfied.

I found out that my girlfriend slept with someone else. She says she doesn't have feelings for him and will never see him again. She said she did it because she was drunk. Should I forgive her?

Not until you find out the real story. I've been plenty drunk and horny before but have still managed to keep my pants on until I could get my hands on my boyfriend. Just think about the number of decisions she made on the way to waking up next to this guy. She must have 1) flirted with him, 2) kissed him, 3) gone someplace private with him, 4) gotten naked, and 5) done the nasty. That's five times she chose to betray your trust and risk ruining her relationship with you. That's no tiny slipup, so there must be a reason why she chose him over you each time. Was she upset with you? Has her confidence been low lately? Does she feel neglected? If you can hash out the underlying problem and solve it, maybe you'll be able to forgive and forget. But if she insists there's nothing wrong, then clearly she's not mature enough to handle a committed relationship and it will probably happen again. Personally, I deal with cheating the way the White House deals with drugs: zero tolerance.

■ Taking the Next Step (or Not)

What do women think about shacking up with a serious boyfriend?

Among my friends there are two opposing schools of thought: 1) Never live together before you get married, because if you're not ready to get married, you aren't ready to live together. 2) Never get married before living together, because you don't really know if you want to marry someone until you've lived with him.

I vote for #2. Living together is a lot of fun, a great way to save money, and the only way to discover if someone's habits and peccadilloes gel with your own. And if you've shared a bed, a bathroom, and the bills successfully, sharing a last name will feel like a natural next step.

Percentage of female college students who agree that it's a good idea to live with someone before deciding to marry him: **53**

(SOURCES: shethinks.org)

Fact: People living together have sex more often than those who are either married or single.

(Durex Global Survey 2001)

How can I tell if we're ready to move in together?

First you need to find out if you agree on what moving in together means. If she thinks it means you're definitely going to get married someday and you think it's just a matter of convenience, you've got a major problem. Another way to figure out if you're ready is to think back to all those times

THE UP SIDE OF SETTLING DOWN
Seven Reasons to Get Serious

1. Being with your significant other lowers your blood pressure more than hanging out with friends or being alone.
2. Nearly three-fifths of married people find sex better or much better after marriage than before.
3. Eighty-nine percent of married men and 83 percent of married women say their spouses are also their best friends.
4. Happily married men live an average of 6 years longer than single men.
5. Two separate polls found that more than 93 percent of married respondents said they felt good about their marriages.
6. Getting married or staying married reduces symptoms of depression.
7. The divorce rate has been steadily dropping since peaking in 1981. In 2000 the divorce rate dropped to its lowest since 1972.

(SOURCES: State University of New York; *The Janus Report on Sexual Behavior*; *The Men's Health Longevity Program*; Patrick McKenry, Ph.D., Ohio State University; 1999 and 2000 Harris Polls; National Center for Health Statistics)

when you haven't agreed on something. What happened? Did you find a way to work it out without too much stress? I hope so because living together is all about compromise—or at the very least taking turns letting each other win. It's also about giving up independence and privacy—she has a right to know where you're going and where you've been, how much money you have in your checking account, and who's calling you at 1:00 A.M. Last, think about the absolute worst aspects of each other's personality. Can you live with each one? If all that sounds okay to both of you, then I guess you're as ready as you'll ever be.

She wants to move in together, but I need more time. How can I keep her from dumping me over this?

She'll dump you only if she thinks you're a lost cause—so give her some hope that you'll be ready in the near(ish) future. Tell her you need 6 months (or longer) to think before you can talk about it again. If your answer is still no at that point, you'll have to explain yourself in more detail. The most girl-friendly reasons would be that you want to reach a certain point in your career or accomplish something else very specific before settling down. If that's the case, she'll understand your hesitation has more to do with your own psyche than any problem with her or the relationship.

If the truth is you're not sure she's right for you, or you feel like you'd be giving up too much of your independence if you shared the same space with her, then be honest with her. She might break up with you out of frustration, but if she really loves you, she's much more likely to be willing to wait if she understands where you're coming from.

How do I know if she's The One?

I'm not sure I believe in "soul mates," but if your relationship meets the following criteria, there's a damn good chance you can keep each other happy for the next 50 years.

- She backs you up no matter your goal—whether it's working out three times a week or changing careers—and wants to help any way she can.

> Percentage of Americans who believe in one true love: **74**
>
> (SOURCE: 2000 Gallup Poll)

- You're honest with each other even when the truth is going to cause problems.
- You spend equal amounts of time listening to each other complain.

- You have fun together doing absolutely nothing.
- You like who you are around her. She makes you a better person.
- Your fights usually spiral down into rational discussions.
- You find her very, very attractive.
- You have crazy, amazing, out-of-this-world sex and neither of you is afraid to suggest new tricks.
- You have the same values when it comes to fidelity, marriage, and family.

Most of my girlfriend's friends are recently engaged or married. After so many weddings and showers, I think she's freaking out about our future. How do I reassure her that I want to be with her without popping the question?

Good news: There's one brilliantly simple thing you can say that will make her incredibly happy while letting her know not to expect a diamond anytime soon. The next time marriage comes up in conversation, tell her in a casual but serious tone that even though you're not ready to tie the knot yet, you think being married to her would be wonderful. She'll be so flattered by the second part of your statement that the first part will go down like honey. If she asks why you're not ready yet, be honest—even if you don't know the answer. The idea that you might look forward to calling her your wife one day will buy you at least another 6 months before she starts getting antsy again.

Average age at which women get married: **25**

Average age at which women have their first child: **24.3**

(SOURCES: U.S. Census Bureau, 2000; National Vital Statistics Report, Vol. 48, No. 3, March 2000)

What is it about weddings that make women obsessed with them?

Just think about it. Women love to plan. We love to pick out dresses, dishes, flowers, and other pretty things. We love to be in control. We love to get attention. We love to look and feel like a princess. Toss it all together on the same day and it's like one heroin rush after another. And not only are we getting high, our mother, sister, and best friends are flying right up there with us.

What do you and your friends consider the key qualities you want in a husband?

Trustworthy is number one for me and all of the women I hang out with, followed by funny, social, patient, accepting, affectionate, kid loving, passionate, open-minded, and fun.

Percentage of women ages 20 to 29 who feel that a husband who can communicate his deepest feelings is more desirable than one who makes a good living: **80**
Percentage of singles who think it's important to find a spouse of the same religious faith: **42**

(source: 2001 Gallup Poll)

What do women want in a marriage proposal? Seems like a guy needs an elaborate gimmick these days.

On one episode of *Sex and the City*, the world's best boyfriend, played by John Corbett, asked Sarah Jessica Parker's character to marry him, and every cable-subscribing woman in the free world gasped and swooned. He took dog and girl out for a walk in the middle of the night and bent down on one knee under the guise of scooping the poop but handed Sarah the ring instead. And then he said the magic words: "I love you and couldn't love anyone more. I want to marry you." It was sweet (albeit stinky), intimate, and absolutely nongimmicky. As a rule, you've got to fit the proposal to the woman. If your girlfriend loves road trips and country music, consider taking her on a drive along the coast, with Johnny Cash wafting from the speakers, before pulling into a scenic overlook and popping the question. If she's nostalgic and you met in a pretty place like a city park or on a ski slope, take her back to the original spot and explain that it was the luckiest moment of your life. Simple but special, that's the idea.

How often do women think about their biological clock? At what age does it start ticking?

More and more often since a book about fertility (*Creating a Life: Professional Women and the Quest for Children* by Sylvia Ann Hewlett) came out in March 2002 and started a media frenzy about how hard it is to have kids after the age of 35. Suddenly those of us who had decided to be chill about it and rely on the wonders of science to get us pregnant at any age got an unpleasant reality check. I have friends as young as 25 who worry that they're not going to meet the right man in time and will end up celebrating their 34th birthday at a sperm bank. It's the weirdest thing to know that if you want to have a traditional family, you have X number of years to fall in love, get married, and start having kids. We may not think about it every day, but it's always in the back of our minds.

GIRLS OVERHEARD:
Keeping Sex Hot

The Scene

Dinner on a weeknight at an uptown restaurant with a great outdoor patio. We're drinking white wine and eating strawberries and whipped cream for dessert—perfect for talking about sex.

The Guest List

Valerie, 28, works for a nonprofit organization and lives with her boyfriend of 2 years

Ellen, 29, a magazine editor, has been dating her boyfriend for 4 years

Reese, 25, a fashion buyer, has been in a long-distance relationship for about a year and a half

Me: I've always thought the best way to keep a relationship sexually charged is to go on vacation together as often as possible and do it everywhere you can along the way.

Valerie: Especially if you get a room with a massive bathtub!

Ellen: My boyfriend and I go camping every few months and do it in the woods, in streams, in the tent. We'll have sex way more than we would at home.

Reese: Because we live on different coasts, we're always meeting in the middle at random destinations, and I think it makes the sex even hotter. We feel like secret agents or criminals on the lam.

Me: What about things you can do at home?

Ellen: You just have to keep trying new things. When you stop doing that, sex gets too predictable.

Valerie: Yeah, you have to surprise each other. The other night, we were walking down a quiet street and he suddenly pressed me up against the wall of a building and started kissing me and grinding his hips against me. He'd never done that before and it really turned me on.

Me: A long-term boyfriend would always make me crazy by licking a different part of my body during sex. One night it was the back of my knees, the next night it was up and down my spine, the next it was my hips.

Reese: I'll pack a new kind of massage oil when I visit him so we have an excuse to start off a night by taking off our clothes and pawing each other from head to toe. More guys need to go to places like the Body Shop and hunt for stuff that could spice up their sex lives.

Ellen: Our sex life had been lagging for a while when Nate reached over and started touching my breasts and rubbing my clitoris while I was driving. That one experience perked things up for months. We started teasing and touching each other everywhere—at the grocery store, in elevators, under the table at restaurants.

Reese: My boyfriend knows that a champagne buzz makes me really horny. He'll order a bottle halfway through dinner and be guaranteed a wild romp that night.

Valerie: I'm a real believer in the ambush. I mean, your biggest fear is that your partner isn't attracted to you anymore, right? And when he literally ambushes you and can't take his hands off you, it's incredible. It helps you know he still thinks you're irresistible.

Me: Someone mentioned massage oil. But what about lube?

That can change everything—it makes everyday sex so much hotter.

Ellen: Lube is amazing. There are so many different kinds out there, and so many different things you can do with it. We didn't start using it until we had been dating for a couple of years, and I wish we had discovered it sooner.

Reese: One of my favorite things is to spend an entire day in bed just fooling around. We do that all the time and it's so luxurious and erotic. We'll just lie there, taking turns going down on each other and feeling each other up. Because you have hours and hours to play, it's less about an ultimate goal and more about having a good time.

Ellen: My boyfriend and I read erotic stories to each other in bed. If you like that kind of thing, it can really rile you up.

Me: What about porn or using sex toys? Do any of you go there?

Reese: We've debated watching porn—every hotel has the pay-per-view stuff—but I've never wanted to. Your average sexy romance flick is great for getting me in the mood, but porn makes me too uncomfortable. As for sex toys, he's going to eventually meet my vibrator and I hope he won't mind using it on me.

Ellen: We sometimes watch adult stuff together—as long as I get to pick the movie. As corny as porn is, watching other people go at it is an instant aphrodisiac. I see it; I want to do it. And we use a vibrator all the time. He likes how it feels when I press it against that area behind his balls. And, naturally, I love it when he uses it on me.

Me: How did you start using it together?

Ellen: Out of the blue one night, he asked me if I owned a vibrator. Then he asked if we could use it together. I was surprised . . . and happy. A vibrator and a man in the same bed? Paradise.

Valerie: We haven't watched porn or used any sex toys together, but I wouldn't rule anything out for the future. Maybe when we're 60 years old, we'll need the extra stimulation.

INDEX

height, 25–26
home, 66–67
intelligence, 76
menstrual cycle, 6–7
playing hard to get, 64, 116
talking (*see* Talk, about)
wealth, 25, 44–45
work (*see* Work)
long-distance, 68
nice guys, 78
psychology of, 64
attraction of opposites, 140
response to, 74, 75
strategies for, 23–24, 47–48,
63–64
test, for compatibility, 140–41
Designated driver, 39
Diary, 10–11
Divorce, dating after, 25
Dogs
jealousy of, 151
men with, 45, 67
as props, 31, 65
Drinking
alcoholic beverages
booty calls after, 88–89
cheating after, 152–53
implications of, 38–39
sex and, 41, 69
nonalcoholic beverages, 39

E

Education, after breakup, 124
Ejaculation, 99
E-mail
address, exchanging, 39–40
after
date, 73–74
first meeting, 40
rejection, 117
sex, 43
replying to, 73–74, 75, 114
Exercise, 28–29. *See also* Gym;
Physical fitness
after breakup, 123–24
with girlfriend, 132
obsession with, 141–42

F

Facial features, your, 27
Fantasies, 11–15, 82–84, 88, 88, 94–95
Fellatio, 5, 94, 96–99, 102, 127
Fighting
about, 136
drinking too much, 137
past relationships, 149
romantic ideals, 135–36, 139–40
smoking, 136
impact of, on relationship, 137
self-defense plan for, 138–39
Flirting, 32, 35–37, 41, 150–51
Flowers, 54, 143, 144
Food
for comfort, 81
on dates, 53, 132, 144
Foreplay
on first dates, 54–56
initiating, 97
kissing as, 55–56, 56, 126
movies for, 147
role-playing as, 104
stopping, 41
Friends
becoming, after breakup, 118–19
female
dating, 38, 78–79, 113–14
flirting while hanging out with,
32
nice guys and, 78
sex with, 13 43, 79–79
introducing girlfriend to male,
81–82

G

Gas, 16, 134
Genital herpes, 69–70
Gibson, Mel, 12
Goatees, 26
Gym
equipment, for sexual excitement,
84
locker room activities at, 20
ogling bodies at, 13–14
working out at, for sex appeal, 28–29
Gynecological exam, 3